REE

in **government**
and **public service**

Diane Lindsey Reeves
with Don Rauf

Ferguson
An imprint of Infobase Publishing

Career Ideas for Teens in Government and Public Service

Copyright © 2005 by Bright Futures Press

Ferguson
An imprint of Infobase Publishing
132 West 31st Street
New York NY 10001

ISBN-10: 0-8160-5292-1
ISBN-13: 978-0-8160-5292-9

Library of Congress Cataloging-in-Publication Data

Reeves, Diane Lindsey, 1959–
Career ideas for teens in government and public service / Diane Lindsey Reeves, with Don Rauf.
   p. cm.
  Includes index.
  ISBN 0-8160-5292-1 (hc : alk. paper)
  1. Civil service positions—United States. 2. Teenagers—Vocational guidance—United States. I. Rauf, Don. II. Title.
JK716.R44 2005
  351.73'023—dc22

2005001356

Ferguson books are available at special discounts when purchased in bulk quantities for businesses, associations, institutions, or sales promotions. Please call our Special Sales Department in New York at (212) 967-8800 or (800) 322-8755.

You can find Ferguson on the World Wide Web at http://www.fergpubco.com

Text design by Joel and Sandy Armstrong
Cover design by Nora Wertz
Illustrations by Matt Wood

Printed in the United States of America

VB PKG 10 9 8 7 6 5 4 3 2

This book is printed on acid-free paper.

contents

acknowledgments

A million thanks to the people who took the time to share their career stories and provide photos for this book:

Bill Atkinson
Michael Britnall
Kimberly Green
Thomas Olson
Robert Rauf
Jim Wagner

And a big thank-you to the contributing writers who helped fill these pages with important and interesting information:

Christen Brownlee
Samantha Henderson
Gail Karlitz
Monique Vescia

career ideas for teens welcome to your future

Q: What's one of the most boring questions adults ask teens?

A: "So . . . what do you want to be when you grow up?"

Well-meaning adults always seem so interested in what you plan to be.

You, on the other hand, are just trying to make it through high school in one piece.

But you may still have a nagging feeling that you really need to find some direction and think about what you want to do with your life.

When it comes to choosing your life's work there's some good news and some bad news. The good news is that, according to the U.S. Bureau of Labor Statistics, you have more than 12,000 different occupations to choose from. With that many options there's got to be something that's just right for you.

Right?

Absolutely.

But . . .

Here comes the bad news.

THERE ARE MORE THAN 12,000 DIFFERENT OCCUPATIONS TO CHOOSE FROM!

How in the world are you ever going to figure out which one is right for you?

We're so glad you asked!

Helping high school students like you make informed choices about their future is what this book (and each of the other titles in the *Career Ideas for Teens* series) is all about. Here you'll encounter 10 tough questions designed to help you answer the biggest one of all: "What in the world am I going to do after I graduate from high school?"

The *Career Ideas for Teens* series enables you to expand your horizons beyond the "doctor, teacher, lawyer" responses common to those new to the career exploration process. The books provide a no-pressure introduction to real jobs that real people do. And they offer a chance to "try on" different career options before committing to a specific college program or career path. Each title in this series is based on one of the 16 career clusters established by the U.S. Department of Education.

And what is a career cluster, you ask? Career clusters are based on a simple and very useful concept. Each cluster consists of all entry-level through professional-level occupations in a broad industry area. All of the jobs and industries in a cluster have many things in common. This organizational structure makes it easier for people like you to get a handle on the big world of work. So instead of rushing headlong into a mind-boggling exploration of the entire universe of career opportunities, you get a chance to tiptoe into smaller, more manageable segments first.

We've used this career cluster concept to organize the *Career Ideas for Teens* series of books. For example, careers related to the arts, communication, and entertainment are organized or "clustered" into the *Career Ideas for Teens in the Arts and Communications* title; a wide variety of health care professions are included in *Career Ideas for Teens in Health Science*; and so on.

Clueless as to what some of these industries are all about? Can't even imagine how something like manufacturing or public administration could possibly relate to you?

No problem.

You're about to find out. Just be prepared to expect the unexpected as you venture out into the world of work. There are some pretty incredible options out there, and some pretty surprising ones too. In fact, it's quite possible that you'll discover that the ideal career for you is one you had never heard of before.

Whatever you do, don't cut yourself short by limiting yourself to just one book in the series. You may find that your initial interests guide you towards the health sciences field—which would, of course, be a good place to start. However, you may discover some new "twists" with a look through the arts and communications book. There you may find a way to blend your medical interests with your exceptional writing and speaking skills by considering becoming a public relations (PR) specialist for a hospital or pharmaceutical company. Or look at the book on education to see about becoming a public health educator or school nurse.

Before you get started, you should know that this book is divided into three sections, each representing an important step toward figuring out what to do with your life.

The first eight titles in the *Career Ideas for Teens* series focus on:

- Architecture and Construction
- Arts and Communications
- Education and Training
- Government and Public Service
- Health Science
- Information Technology
- Law and Public Safety
- Manufacturing

Before You Get Started

Unlike most books, this one is meant to be actively experienced, rather than merely read. Passive perusal won't cut it. Energetic engagement is what it takes to figure out something as important as the rest of your life.

As we've already mentioned, you'll encounter 10 important questions as you work your way through this book. Following each Big Question is an activity designated with a symbol that looks like this:

Every time you see this symbol, you'll know it's time to invest a little energy in your future by getting out your notebook or binder, a pen or pencil, and doing whatever the instructions direct you to do. If this book is your personal property, you can choose to do the activities right in the book. But you still might want to make copies of your finished products to go in a binder so they are all in one place for easy reference.

When you've completed all the activities, you'll have your own personal **Big Question AnswerBook**, a planning guide representing a straightforward and truly effective process you can use throughout your life to make fully informed career decisions.

discover you at work

This first section focuses on a very important subject: You. It poses four Big Questions that are designed specifically to help you "discover you":

? Big Question #1: **who are you?**
? Big Question #2: **what are your interests and strengths?**
? Big Question #3: **what are your work values?**

Then, using an interest assessment tool developed by the U.S. Department of Labor and implemented with your very vivid imagination, you'll picture yourself doing some of the things that people actually do for their jobs. In other words, you'll start "discovering you at work" by answering the following:

? Big Question #4: **what's your work personality?**

Unfortunately, this first step is often a misstep for many people. Or make that a "missed" step. When you talk with the adults in your life about their career choices, you're likely to find that some of them never even considered the idea of choosing a career based on personal preferences and strengths. You're also likely to learn that if they had it to do over again, this step would definitely play a significant role in the choices they would make.

explore your options

There's more than meets the eye when it comes to finding the best career to pursue. There are also countless ways to blend talent or passion in these areas in some rather unexpected and exciting ways. Get ready to find answers to two more Big Questions as you browse through an entire section of career profiles:

? Big Question #5: **do you have the right skills?**
? Big Question #6: **are you on the right path?**

experiment with success

At long last you're ready to give this thing called career planning a trial run. Here's where you'll encounter three Big Questions that will unleash critical decision-making strategies and skills that will serve you well throughout a lifetime of career success.

While you're at it, take some time to sit in on a roundtable discussion with successful professionals representing a very impressive array of careers related to this industry. Many of their experiences will apply to your own life, even if you don't plan to pursue the same careers.

? Big Question #7: **who knows what you need to know?**
? Big Question #8: **how can you find out what a career is really like?**
? Big Question #9: **how do you know when you've made the right choice?**

Then as you begin to pull all your new insights and ideas together, you'll come to one final question:

? Big Question #10: **what's next?**

As you get ready to take the plunge, remember that this is a book about possibilities and potential. You can use it to make the most of your future work!

Here's what you'll need to complete the Big Question AnswerBook:

- A notebook or binder for the completed activities included in all three sections of the book
- An openness to new ideas
- Complete and completely candid answers to the 10 Big Question activities

So don't just read it, do it.
Plan it.
Dream it.

SECTION 1

discover you at work

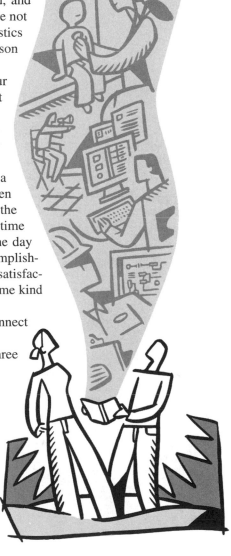

The goal here is to get some clues about who you are and what you should do with your life.
As time goes by, you will grow older, become more educated, and have more experiences, but many things that truly define you are not likely to change. Even now you possess very strong characteristics —genuine qualities that mark you as the unique and gifted person that you undoubtedly are.

It's impossible to overestimate the importance of giving your wholehearted attention to this step. You, after all, are the most valuable commodity you'll ever have to offer a future employer. Finding work that makes the most of your assets often means the difference between enjoying a rewarding career and simply earning a paycheck.

You've probably already experienced the satisfaction of a good day's work. You know what we mean—those days when you get all your assignments in on time, you're prepared for the pop quiz your teacher sprung on you, and you beat your best time during sports practice. You may be exhausted at the end of the day but you can't help but feel good about yourself and your accomplishments. A well-chosen career can provide that same sense of satisfaction. Since you're likely to spend upwards of 40 years doing some kind of work, well-informed choices make a lot of sense!

Let's take a little time for you to understand yourself and connect what you discover about yourself to the world of work.

To find a career path that's right for you, we'll tackle these three Big Questions first:

- **who are you?**
- **what are your interests and strengths?**
- **what are your work values?**

? Big Question #1:
who are you?

Have you ever noticed how quickly new students in your school or new families in your community find the people who are most like them? If you've ever been the "new" person yourself, you've probably spent your first few days sizing up the general population and then getting in with the people who dress in clothes a lot like yours, appreciate the same style of music, or maybe even root for the same sports teams.

Given that this process happens so naturally—if not necessarily on purpose—it should come as no surprise that many people lean toward jobs that surround them with people most like them. When people with common interests, common values, and complementary talents come together in the workplace, the results can be quite remarkable.

Many career aptitude tests, including the one developed by the U.S. Department of Labor and included later in this book, are based on the theory that certain types of people do better at certain types of jobs. It's like a really sophisticated matchmaking service. Take your basic strengths and interests and match them to the strengths and interests required by specific occupations.

It makes sense when you think about it. When you want to find a career that's ideally suited for you, find out what people like you are doing and head off in that direction!

There's just one little catch.

The only way to recognize other people like you is to recognize yourself. Who are you anyway? What are you like? What's your basic approach to life and work?

Now's as good a time as any to find out. Let's start by looking at who you are in a systematic way. This process will ultimately help you understand how to identify personally appropriate career options.

Big Activity #1:
who are you?

On a sheet of paper, if this book doesn't belong to you, create a list of adjectives that best describe you. You should be able to come up with at least 15 qualities that apply to you. There's no need to make judgments about whether these qualities are good or bad. They just are. They represent who you are and can help you understand what you bring to the workforce.

(If you get stuck, ask a trusted friend or adult to help describe especially strong traits they see in you.)

Some of the types of qualities you may choose to include are:

- **How you relate to others:**
  Are you shy? Outgoing? Helpful? Dependent? Empathic? In charge? Agreeable? Challenging? Persuasive? Popular? Impatient? A loner?
- **How you approach new situations:**
  Are you adventurous? Traditional? Cautious? Enthusiastic? Curious?
- **How you feel about change—planned or unplanned:**
  Are you resistant? Adaptable? Flexible? Predictable?
- **How you approach problems:**
  Are you persistent? Spontaneous? Methodical? Creative?
- **How you make decisions:**
  Are you intuitive? Logical? Emotional? Practical? Systematic? Analytical?
- **How you approach life:**
  Are you laid back? Ambitious? Perfectionist? Idealistic? Optimistic? Pessimistic? Self-sufficient?

Feel free to use any of these words if they happen to describe you well, but please don't limit yourself to this list. Pick the best adjectives that paint an accurate picture of the real you. Get more ideas from a dictionary or thesaurus if you'd like.

When you're finished, put the completed list in your Big Question AnswerBook.

Big Activity #1: **who are you?**

fifteen qualities that describe me		
1	2	3
4	5	6
7	8	9
10	11	12
13	14	15
etc.		

Big Question #2:
what are your interests and strengths?

For many people, doing something they like to do is the most important part of deciding on a career path—even more important than how much money they can earn!

We don't all like to do the same things—and that's good. For some people, the ideal vacation is lying on a beach, doing absolutely nothing; others would love to spend weeks visiting museums and historic places. Some people wish they had time to learn to skydive or fly a plane; others like to learn to cook gourmet meals or do advanced math.

If we all liked the same things, the world just wouldn't work very well. There would be incredible crowds in some places and ghost towns in others. Some of our natural resources would be overburdened; others would never be used. We would all want to eat at the same restaurant, wear the same outfit, see the same movie, and live in the same place. How boring!

So let's get down to figuring out what you most like to do and how you can spend your working life doing just that. In some ways your answer to this question is all you really need to know about choosing a career, because the people who enjoy their work the most are those who do something they enjoy. We're not talking rocket science here. Just plain old common sense.

Big Activity # 2:
what are your interests and strengths?

Imagine this: No school, no job, no homework, no chores, no obligations at all. All the time in the world you want to do all the things you like most. You know what we're talking about—those things that completely grab your interest and keep you engrossed for hours without your getting bored. Those kinds of things you do really well—sometimes effortlessly, sometimes with extraordinary (and practiced) skill.

And, by the way, EVERYONE has plenty of both interests and strengths. Some are just more visible than others.

Step 1: Write the three things you most enjoy doing on a sheet of paper, if this book doesn't belong to you. Leave lots of space after each thing.

Step 2: Think about some of the deeper reasons why you enjoy each of these activities—the motivations beyond "it's fun." Do you enjoy shopping because it gives you a chance to be with your friends? Because it allows you to find new ways to express your individuality? Because you enjoy the challenge of finding bargains or things no one else has discovered? Or because it's fun to imagine the lifestyle you'll be able to lead when you're finally rich and famous? In the blank spaces, record the reasons why you enjoy each activity.

Step 3: Keep this list handy in your Big Question AnswerBook so that you can refer to it any time you have to make a vocational decision. Sure, you may have to update the list from time to time as your interests change. But one thing is certain. The kind of work you'll most enjoy will be linked in some way to the activities on that list. Count on it.

Maybe one of your favorite things to do is "play basketball." Does that mean the only way you'll ever be happy at work is to play professional basketball?

Maybe.

Maybe not.

Use your *why* responses to read between the lines. The *whys* can prove even more important than the *whats*. Perhaps what you like most about playing basketball is the challenge or the chance to be part of a team that shares a common goal. Maybe you really like pushing yourself to improve. Or it could be the rush associated with competition and the thrill of winning.

The more you uncover your own *whys*, the closer you'll be to discovering important clues about the kinds of work that are best for you.

Big Activity #2: **what are your interests and strengths?**

things you enjoy doing	why you enjoy doing them
1	• • •
2	• • •
3	• • •

Big Question #3:
what are your work values?

Chances are, you've never given a moment's thought to this next question. At least not in the context of career planning.

You already looked at who you are and what you enjoy and do well. The idea being, of course, to seek out career options that make the most of your innate qualities, preferences, and natural abilities.

As you start checking into various careers, you'll discover one more dimension associated with making personally appropriate career choices. You'll find that even though people may have the exact same job title, they may execute their jobs in dramatically different ways. For instance, everyone knows about teachers. They teach things to other people. Period.

But wait. If you line up 10 aspiring teachers in one room, you may be surprised to discover how vastly different their interpretations of the job may be. There are the obvious differences, of course. One may want to teach young children; one may want to teach adults. One will focus on teaching math, while another one focuses on teaching Spanish.

Look a little closer and you'll find even greater disparity in the choices they make. One may opt for the prestige (and paycheck) of working in an Ivy League college, while another is completely committed to teaching disadvantaged children in a remote area of the Appalachian Mountains. One may approach teaching simply as a way to make a living, while another devotes almost every waking hour to working with his or her students.

These subtle but significant differences reflect what's truly important to each person. In a word, they reflect the person's values—those things that are most important to them.

People's values depend on many factors—their upbringing, their life experiences, their goals and ambitions, their religious beliefs, and, quite frankly, the way they view the world and their role in it. Very few people share exactly the same values. However, that doesn't necessarily mean that some people are right and others are wrong. It just means they have different perspectives.

Here's a story that shows how different values can be reflected in career choices.

Imagine: It's five years after college graduation and a group of college friends are back together for the first time. They catch up about their lives, their families, and their careers. Listen in on one of their reunion conversations and see if you can guess what each is doing now.

Alice: I have the best career. Every day I get the chance to help kids with special needs get a good education.

Bob: I love my career, too. It's great to know that I am making my town a safer place for everyone.

Cathy: It was tough for me to commit to more school after college. But I'm glad I did. After all I went through when my parents divorced, I'm glad I can be there to make things easier for other families.

David: I know how you feel. I'm glad I get to do something that helps companies function smoothly and keep our economy strong. Of course, you remember that I had a hard time deciding whether to pursue this career or teaching! This way I get the best of both worlds.

Elizabeth: It's great that we both ended up in the corporate world. You know that I was always intrigued by the stock market.

So exactly what is each of the five former freshman friends doing today? Have you made your guesses?

Alice is a lawyer. She specializes in education law. She makes sure that school districts provide special needs children with all of the resources they are entitled to under the law.

Bob is a lawyer. He is a prosecuting attorney and makes his town safer by ensuring that justice is served when someone commits a crime.

Cathy is a lawyer. She practices family law. She helps families negotiate separation and divorce agreements and makes sure that adoption and custody proceedings protect everyone involved. Sometimes she even provides legal intervention to protect adults or children who are in abusive situations.

David is a lawyer. He practices employment law. He helps companies set up policies that follow fair employment practices. He also gives seminars to managers, teaching them what the law says and means about sexual harassment, discrimination, and termination of employment.

Elizabeth is a lawyer. She practices corporate law and is indispensable to corporations with legal responsibilities towards stockholders and the government.

Wow! All five friends have the same job title. But each describes his/her job so differently! All five were able to enter the field of law and focus on the things that are most important to them: quality education, freedom from crime, protection of families and children, fairness in the workplace, and corporate economic growth. Identifying and honoring your personal values is an important part of choosing your life's work.

Big Activity #3:
what are your work values?

Step 1: Look at the following chart. If this book doesn't belong to you, divide a sheet of paper into the following three columns:

● **Essential**

Statements that fall into this column are very important to you. If the job doesn't satisfy these needs, you're not interested.

● **Okay**

Great if the job satisfies these needs, but you can also live without them.

● **No Way**

Statements that fall into this column represent needs that are not at all important to you or things you'd rather do without or simply couldn't tolerate.

Step 2: Look over the following list of statements representing different work values. Rewrite each statement in the appropriate column. Does the first statement represent something that is critical to you to have in your work? If so, write it in the first column. No big deal either way? Write it in the second column. Couldn't stand it? Write it in the third column. Repeat the same process for each of the value statements.

Step 3: When you're finished, place your complete work values chart in your Big Question AnswerBook.

Got it? Then get with it.

Really think about these issues. Lay it on the line. What values are so deeply ingrained in you that you'd be absolutely miserable if you had to sacrifice them for a job? Religious beliefs and political leanings fall into this category for some people.

Which ones provide room for some give and take? Things like vacation and benefits, working hours, and other issues along those lines may be completely negotiable for some people, but absolutely not for others.

Just remember, wherever you go and whatever you do, be sure that the choices you make are true to you.

Big Activity #3: **what are your work values?**

work values	essential	okay	no way
1. I can count on plenty of opportunity for advancement and taking on more responsibility.			
2. I can work to my fullest potential using all of my abilities.			
3. I would be able to give directions and instructions to others.			
4. I would always know exactly what my manager expects of me.			
5. I could structure my own day.			
6. I would be very busy all day.			
7. I would work in attractive and pleasant surroundings.			
8. My coworkers would be people I might choose as friends.			
9. I would get frequent feedback about my performance.			
10. I could continue my education to progress to an even higher level job.			
11. Most of the time I would be able to work alone.			
12. I would know precisely what I need to do to succeed at the job.			
13. I could make decisions on my own.			

Big Activity #3: **what are your work values?**

work values	essential	okay	no way
14. I would have more than the usual amount of vacation time.			
15. I would be working doing something I really believe in.			
16. I would feel like part of a team.			
17. I would find good job security and stable employment opportunities in the industry.			
18. I could depend on my manager for the training I need.			
19. I would earn lots of money.			
20. I would feel a sense of accomplishment in my work.			
21. I would be helping other people.			
22. I could try out my own ideas.			
23. I would not need to have further training or education to do this job.			
24. I would get to travel a lot.			
25. I could work the kind of hours I need to balance work, family, and personal responsibilities.			

To summarize in my own words, the work values most important to me include:

Big Question #4: what is your work personality?

Congratulations. After completing the first three activities, you've already discovered a set of skills you can use throughout your life. Basing key career decisions on factors associated with who you are, what you enjoy and do well, and what's most important about work will help you today as you're just beginning to explore the possibilities, as well as into the future as you look for ways to cultivate your career.

Now that you've got that mastered, let's move on to another important skill. This one blends some of what you just learned about yourself with what you need to learn about the real world of work. It's a reality check of sorts as you align and merge your personal interests and abilities with those required in different work situations. At the end of this task you will identify your personal interest profile.

This activity is based on the work of Dr. John Holland. Dr. Holland conducted groundbreaking research that identified different characteristics in people. He found that he could classify people into six basic groups based on which characteristics tended to occur at the same time. He also found that the characteristics that defined the different groups of people were also characteristics that corresponded to success in different groups of occupations. The result of all that work was a classification system that identifies and names six distinct groups of people who share personal interests or characteristics and are likely to be successful in a group of clearly identified jobs.

Dr. Holland's work is respected by workforce professionals everywhere and is widely used by employers and employment agencies to help people get a handle on the best types of work to pursue.

The following Work Interest Profiler (WIP) is based on Dr. Holland's theories and was developed by the U.S. Department of Labor's Employment and Training Administration as part of an important project called O*Net. O*Net is a system used in all 50 states to provide career and employment services to thousands of people every year. It's a system you'll want to know about when it's time to take that first plunge into the world of work. If you'd like, you can find more information about this system at **http://online.onetcenter.org**.

Big Activity #4:
what is your work personality?

By completing O*Net's Work Interest Profiler (WIP), you'll gain valuable insight into the types of work that are right for you.

here's how it works

The WIP lists many activities that real people do at real jobs. Your task is to read a brief statement about each of these activities and decide if it is something you think you'd enjoy doing. Piece of cake!

Don't worry about whether you have enough education or training to perform the activity. And, for now, forget about how much money you would make performing the activity.

Just boil it down to whether or not you'd like performing each work activity. If you'd like it, put a check in the *like* column that corresponds to each of the six interest areas featured in the test on the handy dandy chart you're about to create (or use the one in the book if it's yours). If you don't like it, put that check in the *dislike* column. What if you don't have a strong opinion on a particular activity? That's okay. Count that one as *unsure*.

Be completely honest with yourself. No one else is going to see your chart. If you check things you think you "should" check, you are not helping yourself find the career that will make you happy.

Before you start, create a chart for yourself. Your scoring sheet will have six horizontal rows and three vertical columns. Label the six rows as Sections 1 through 6, and label the three columns *like*, *dislike*, and *unsure*.

how to complete the Work Interest Profiler

Step 1: Start with Section 1.

Step 2: Look at the first activity and decide whether you would like to do it as part of your job.

Step 3: Put a mark in the appropriate column (*Like*, *Dislike*, or *Unsure*) on the Section 1 row.

Step 4: Continue for every activity in Section 1. Then do Sections 2 through 6.

Step 5: When you've finished all of the sections, count the number of marks you have in each column and write down the total.

Remember, this is not a test! There are no right or wrong answers. You are completing this profile to learn more about yourself and your work-related interests.

Also, once you've completed this activity, be sure to put your chart and any notes in your Big Question AnswerBook.

Ready? Let's go!

Section 1

1. Drive a taxi
2. Repair household appliances
3. Catch fish as a member of a fishing crew
4. Paint houses
5. Assemble products in a factory
6. Install flooring in houses
7. Perform lawn care services
8. Drive a truck to deliver packages to homes and offices
9. Work on an offshore oil-drilling rig
10. Put out forest fires
11. Fix a broken faucet
12. Refinish furniture
13. Guard money in an armored car
14. Lay brick or tile
15. Operate a dairy farm
16. Raise fish in a fish hatchery
17. Build a brick walkway
18. Enforce fish and game laws
19. Assemble electronic parts
20. Build kitchen cabinets
21. Maintain the grounds of a park
22. Operate a motorboat to carry passengers
23. Set up and operate machines to make products
24. Spray trees to prevent the spread of harmful insects
25. Monitor a machine on an assembly line

Section 2

1. Study space travel
2. Develop a new medicine
3. Study the history of past civilizations
4. Develop a way to better predict the weather
5. Determine the infection rate of a new disease
6. Study the personalities of world leaders
7. Investigate the cause of a fire
8. Develop psychological profiles of criminals
9. Study whales and other types of marine life
10. Examine blood samples using a microscope
11. Invent a replacement for sugar
12. Study genetics
13. Do research on plants or animals
14. Study weather conditions
15. Investigate crimes
16. Study ways to reduce water pollution
17. Develop a new medical treatment or procedure
18. Diagnose and treat sick animals
19. Conduct chemical experiments
20. Study rocks and minerals
21. Do laboratory tests to identify diseases
22. Study the structure of the human body
23. Plan a research study
24. Study the population growth of a city
25. Make a map of the bottom of the ocean

Section 3

1. Paint sets for a play
2. Create special effects for movies
3. Write reviews of books or movies
4. Compose or arrange music
5. Design artwork for magazines
6. Pose for a photographer
7. Create dance routines for a show
8. Play a musical instrument
9. Edit movies
10. Sing professionally
11. Announce a radio show
12. Perform stunts for a movie or television show
13. Design sets for plays
14. Act in a play
15. Write a song
16. Perform jazz or tap dance
17. Sing in a band
18. Direct a movie
19. Write scripts for movies or television shows
20. Audition singers and musicians for a musical show
21. Conduct a musical choir
22. Perform comedy routines in front of an audience
23. Dance in a Broadway show
24. Perform as an extra in movies, plays, or television shows
25. Write books or plays

Section 4

1. Teach children how to play sports
2. Help people with family-related problems
3. Teach an individual an exercise routine
4. Perform nursing duties in a hospital
5. Help people with personal or emotional problems
6. Teach work and living skills to people with disabilities
7. Assist doctors in treating patients
8. Work with juveniles on probation
9. Supervise the activities of children at a camp
10. Teach an elementary school class
11. Perform rehabilitation therapy
12. Help elderly people with their daily activities
13. Help people who have problems with drugs or alcohol
14. Teach a high school class
15. Give career guidance to people
16. Do volunteer work at a non-profit organization
17. Help families care for ill relatives
18. Teach sign language to people with hearing disabilities
19. Help people with disabilities improve their daily living skills
20. Help conduct a group therapy session
21. Work with children with mental disabilities
22. Give CPR to someone who has stopped breathing
23. Provide massage therapy to people
24. Plan exercises for patients with disabilities
25. Counsel people who have a life-threatening illness

Section 5

1. Sell CDs and tapes at a music store
2. Manage a clothing store
3. Sell houses
4. Sell computer equipment in a store
5. Operate a beauty salon or barber shop
6. Sell automobiles
7. Represent a client in a lawsuit
8. Negotiate business contracts
9. Sell a soft drink product line to stores and restaurants
10. Start your own business
11. Be responsible for the operations of a company
12. Give a presentation about a product you are selling
13. Buy and sell land
14. Sell restaurant franchises to individuals
15. Manage the operations of a hotel
16. Negotiate contracts for professional athletes
17. Sell merchandise at a department store
18. Market a new line of clothing
19. Buy and sell stocks and bonds
20. Sell merchandise over the telephone
21. Run a toy store
22. Sell hair-care products to stores and salons
23. Sell refreshments at a movie theater
24. Manage a retail store
25. Sell telephone and other communication equipment

Section 6

1. Develop an office filing system
2. Generate the monthly payroll checks for an office
3. Proofread records or forms
4. Schedule business conferences
5. Enter information into a database
6. Photocopy letters and reports
7. Keep inventory records
8. Record information from customers applying for charge accounts
9. Load computer software into a large computer network
10. Use a computer program to generate customer bills
11. Develop a spreadsheet using computer software
12. Operate a calculator
13. Direct or transfer office phone calls
14. Use a word processor to edit and format documents
15. Transfer funds between banks, using a computer
16. Compute and record statistical and other numerical data
17. Stamp, sort, and distribute office mail
18. Maintain employee records
19. Record rent payments
20. Keep shipping and receiving records
21. Keep accounts payable/receivable for an office
22. Type labels for envelopes and packages
23. Calculate the wages of employees
24. Take notes during a meeting
25. Keep financial records

Section 1
Realistic

	Like	Dislike	Unsure
1.			
2.			
3.			
4.			
5.			
6.			
7.			
8.			
9.			
10.			
11.			
12.			
13.			
14.			
15.			
16.			
17.			
18.			
19.			
20.			
21.			
22.			
23.			
24.			
25.			

Total Realistic

Section 2
Investigative

	Like	Dislike	Unsure
1.			
2.			
3.			
4.			
5.			
6.			
7.			
8.			
9.			
10.			
11.			
12.			
13.			
14.			
15.			
16.			
17.			
18.			
19.			
20.			
21.			
22.			
23.			
24.			
25.			

Total Investigative

Section 3
Artistic

	Like	Dislike	Unsure
1.			
2.			
3.			
4.			
5.			
6.			
7.			
8.			
9.			
10.			
11.			
12.			
13.			
14.			
15.			
16.			
17.			
18.			
19.			
20.			
21.			
22.			
23.			
24.			
25.			

Total Artistic

Section 4
Social

	Like	Dislike	Unsure
1.			
2.			
3.			
4.			
5.			
6.			
7.			
8.			
9.			
10.			
11.			
12.			
13.			
14.			
15.			
16.			
17.			
18.			
19.			
20.			
21.			
22.			
23.			
24.			
25.			

Total Social

Section 5
Enterprising

	Like	Dislike	Unsure
1.			
2.			
3.			
4.			
5.			
6.			
7.			
8.			
9.			
10.			
11.			
12.			
13.			
14.			
15.			
16.			
17.			
18.			
19.			
20.			
21.			
22.			
23.			
24.			
25.			

Total Enterprising

Section 6
Conventional

	Like	Dislike	Unsure
1.			
2.			
3.			
4.			
5.			
6.			
7.			
8.			
9.			
10.			
11.			
12.			
13.			
14.			
15.			
16.			
17.			
18.			
19.			
20.			
21.			
22.			
23.			
24.			
25.			

Total Conventional

What are your top three work personalities? List them here if this is your own book or on a separate piece of paper if it's not.

1. _____
2. _____
3. _____

all done? let's see what it means

Be sure you count up the number of marks in each column on your scoring sheet and write down the total for each column. You will probably notice that you have a lot of *likes* for some sections, and a lot of *dislikes* for other sections. The section that has the most *likes* is your primary interest area. The section with the next highest number of *likes* is your second interest area. The next highest is your third interest area.

Now that you know your top three interest areas, what does it mean about your work personality type? We'll get to that in a minute, but first we are going to answer a couple of other questions that might have crossed your mind:

- What is the best work personality to have?
- What does my work personality mean?

First of all, there is no "best" personality in general. There is, however, a "best" personality for each of us. It's who we really are and how we feel most comfortable. There may be several "best" work personalities for any job because different people may approach the job in different ways. But there is no "best work personality."

Asking about the "best work personality" is like asking whether the "best" vehicle is a sports car, a sedan, a station wagon, or a sports utility vehicle. It all depends on who you are and what you need.

One thing we do know is that our society needs all of the work personalities in order to function effectively. Fortunately, we usually seem to have a good mix of each type.

So, while many people may find science totally boring, there are many other people who find it fun and exciting. Those are the people who invent new technologies, who become doctors and researchers, and who turn natural resources into the things we use every day. Many people may think that spending a day with young children is unbearable, but those who love that environment are the teachers, community leaders, and museum workers that nurture children's minds and personalities.

When everything is in balance, there's a job for every person and a person for every job.

Now we'll get to your work personality. Following are descriptions of each of Dr. Holland's six work personalities that correspond to the six sections in your last exercise. You, like most people, are a unique combination of more than one. A little of this, a lot of that. That's what makes us interesting.

Identify your top three work personalities. Also, pull out your responses to the first three exercises we did. As you read about your top three work personalities, see how they are similar to the way you described yourself earlier.

Type 1
Realistic

Realistic people are often seen as the "Doers." They have mechanical or athletic ability and enjoy working outdoors.

Realistic people like work activities that include practical, hands-on problems and solutions. They enjoy dealing with plants, animals, and real-life materials like wood, tools, and machinery.

Careers that involve a lot of paperwork or working closely with others are usually not attractive to realistic people.

Who you are:
independent
reserved
practical
mechanical
athletic
persistent

What you like to do/what you do well:
build things
train animals
play a sport
fix things
garden
hunt or fish
woodworking

repair cars
refinish furniture

Career possibilities:
aerospace engineer
aircraft pilot
animal breeder
architect
baker/chef
building inspector
carpenter
chemical engineer
civil engineer
construction manager
dental assistant
detective
glazier
jeweler
machinist
oceanographer
optician
park ranger
plumber
police officer
practical nurse
private investigator
radiologist
sculptor

Type 2
Investigative

Investigative people are often seen as the "Thinkers." They much prefer searching for facts and figuring out problems mentally to doing physical activity or leading other people.

If Investigative is one of your strong interest areas, your answers to the earlier exercises probably matched some of these:

Who you are:
curious
logical
independent
analytical
observant
inquisitive

What you like to do/what you do well:
think abstractly
solve problems
use a microscope
do research
fly a plane
explore new subjects
study astronomy
do puzzles
work with a computer

Career possibilities:

aerospace engineer
archaeologist
CAD technician
chemist
chiropractor
computer programmer
coroner
dentist
electrician
ecologist
geneticist
hazardous waste technician
historian
horticulturist
management consultant
medical technologist
meteorologist
nurse practitioner
pediatrician
pharmacist
political scientist
psychologist
software engineer
surgeon
technical writer
veterinarian
zoologist

Type 3
Artistic

Artistic people are the "Creators." People with this primary interest like work activities that deal with the artistic side of things.

Artistic people need to have the opportunity for self-expression in their work. They want to be able to use their imaginations and prefer to work in less structured environments, without clear sets of rules about how things should be done.

Who you are:
imaginative
intuitive
expressive
emotional
creative
independent

What you like to do/what you do well:
draw
paint
play an instrument
visit museums
act
design clothes or rooms
read fiction
travel
write stories, poetry, or music

Career possibilities:

architect
actor
animator
art director
cartoonist
choreographer
costume designer
composer
copywriter
dancer
disc jockey
drama teacher
emcee
fashion designer
graphic designer
illustrator
interior designer
journalist
landscape architect
medical illustrator
photographer
producer
scriptwriter
set designer

Type 4
Social

Social people are known as the "Helpers." They are interested in work that can assist others and promote learning and personal development.

Communication with other people is very important to those in the Social group. They usually do not enjoy jobs that require a great amount of work with objects, machines, or data. Social people like to teach, give advice, help, cure, or otherwise be of service to people.

Who you are:
friendly
outgoing
empathic
persuasive
idealistic
generous

What you like to do/what you do well:
teach others
work in groups
play team sports
care for children
go to parties
help or advise others
meet new people
express yourself
join clubs or organizations

Career possibilities:
animal trainer
arbitrator
art teacher
art therapist
audiologist
child care worker
clergy person
coach
counselor/therapist
cruise director
dental hygienist
employment interviewer
EMT worker
fitness trainer
flight attendant
occupational therapist
police officer
recreational therapist
registered nurse
school psychologist
social worker
substance abuse counselor
teacher
tour guide

Type 5
Enterprising

Enterprising work personalities can be called the "Persuaders." These people like work activities that have to do with starting up and carrying out projects, especially business ventures. They like taking risks for profit, enjoy being responsible for making decisions, and generally prefer action to thought or analysis.

People in the Enterprising group like to work with other people. While the Social group focuses on helping other people, members of the Enterprising group are able to lead, manage, or persuade other people to accomplish the goals of the organization.

Who you are:
assertive
self-confident
ambitious
extroverted
optimistic
adventurous

What you like to do/what you do well:
organize activities
sell things
promote ideas

discuss politics
hold office in clubs
give talks or speeches
meet people
initiate projects
start your own business

Career possibilities:
advertising
chef
coach, scout
criminal investigator
economist
editor
foreign service officer
funeral director
hotel manager
journalist
lawyer
lobbyist
public relations specialist
newscaster
restaurant manager
sales manager
school principal
ship's captain
stockbroker
umpire, referee
urban planner

Type 6
Conventional

People in the Conventional group are the "Organizers." They like work activities that follow set procedures and routines. They are more comfortable and proficient working with data and detail than they are with generalized ideas.

Conventional people are happiest in work situations where the lines of authority are clear, where they know exactly what responsibilities are expected of them, and where there are precise standards for the work.

Who you are:
well-organized
accurate
practical
persistent
conscientious
ambitious

What you like to do/what you do well:
work with numbers
type accurately
collect or organize things
follow up on tasks
be punctual
be responsible for details
proofread

keep accurate records
understand regulations

Career possibilities:
accountant
actuary
air traffic controller
assessor
budget analyst
building inspector
chief financial officer
corporate treasurer
cost estimator
court reporter
economist
environmental compliance lawyer
fire inspector
insurance underwriter
legal secretary
mathematician
medical secretary
proofreader
tax preparer

government and public service careers work personality codes

Once you've discovered your own unique work personality code, you can use it to explore the careers profiled in this book and elsewhere. Do keep in mind though that this code is just a tool meant to help focus your search. It's not meant to box you in or to keep you from pursuing any career that happens to capture your imagination.

Following is a chart listing the work personality codes associated with each of the careers profiled in this book.

	Realistic	Investigative	Artistic	Social	Enterprising	Conventional
My Work Personality Code (mark your top three areas)						
Air Marshal	X			X	X	
Air Traffic Controller	X			X	X	
Budget Analyst	X				X	X
City Manager				X	X	X
Congressional Aide				X	X	X
Conservationist	X	X		X		
Cryptographer		X	X		X	
Customs and Border Protection Officer	X			X	X	
Development Director			X	X	X	
Ecologist	X			X	X	
Economic Development Director			X	X	X	
Election Supervisor			X	X	X	
Emergency Services Coordinator	X			X	X	
FBI Special Agent	X			X	X	
Firefighter	X			X	X	
Food and Drug Scientist			X	X	X	

My Work Personality Code	Realistic	Investigative	Artistic	Social	Enterprising	Conventional
Foreign Service Officer			X	X	X	
Immigration Agent	X			X	X	
Intelligence Analyst		X	X		X	
IRS (Internal Revenue Service) Agent	X	X				X
Lobbyist			X	X	X	
Media Relations Specialist			X	X	X	
Meteorologist	X	X		X		
Military Serviceperson	*	*	*	*	*	*
Park Ranger	X			X	X	
Police Officer			X	X	X	
Politician		X		X	X	
Postal Service Worker				X	X	X
Public Administrator			X	X	X	
Public Attorney		X		X	X	
Public Health Official		X		X	X	
Public Policy Advisor			X	X	X	
Social Worker			X	X	X	
Transportation Manager	X			X	X	
Urban Planner		X		X	X	

* Varies by Military Occupational Specialty (MOS)

Now it's time to move on to the next big step in the Big Question process. While the first step focused on you, the next one focuses on the world of work. It includes profiles of a wide variety of occupations related to government and public service, a roundtable discussion with professionals working in these fields, and a mind-boggling list of other careers to consider when wanting to blend passion or talent in these areas with your life's work.

explore your options

By now you probably have a fairly good understanding of the assets (some fully realized and perhaps others only partially developed) that you bring to your future career. You've defined key characteristics about yourself, identified special interests and strengths, examined your work values, and analyzed your basic work personality traits. All in all, you've taken a good, hard look at yourself and we're hoping that you're encouraged by all the potential you've discovered.

Now it's time to look at the world of work as it pertains to government and public service. People living in a democratic society are affected by government in countless ways. Everything from the roads we drive on to the courts that enforce our laws are part of the governmental infrastructure.

According to the Partnership for Public Service, a nonprofit organization working to make government an employer of choice for talented, dedicated Americans, "in the last decade, old realities have given way to new circumstances that demand a higher level of performance from our government. Whether it is the continuing effort to protect our homeland, the promotion of a sound economy, or the stewardship of our natural resources, our government institutions are being seriously tested." Success in meeting these challenges rests entirely on bringing the best available talent into the nation's government and public service institutions and managing them well.

Uncle Sam, as the federal government is sometimes fondly called, is one of the nation's largest employers. Add state and local governments to the mix and you'll find a dizzying array of opportunities. Given projections that jobs in state and local governments are expected to increase by 12 percent within the next decade, it is fair to say that opportunities are expected to be plentiful. This factor, coupled with the trend of retiring baby boomers leaving the government workforce in droves over the next 10 to 20 years makes government and public service an industry worthy of your serious consideration.

All the careers generally associated with government and public service can be grouped into seven distinct categories: governance, national security, foreign service, planning, revenue and taxation, regulation, and public management and administration. Understanding these pathways provides important clues about which direction might be best for you. Following are details about each pathway.

fyi Each of the following profiles includes several common elements to help guide you through an effective career exploration process. For each career, you'll find

- A sidebar loaded with information you can use to find out more about the profession. Professional associations, pertinent reading materials, the lowdown on wages and suggested training requirements, and a list of typical types of employers are all included to give you a broader view of what the career is all about.
- An informative essay describing what the career involves.
- Get Started Now strategies you can use right now to get prepared,

test the waters, and develop your skills.
- A Hire Yourself project providing realistic activities like those you would actually find on the job. Try these learning activities and find out what it's really like to be a . . . you name it.

You don't have to read the profiles in order. You may want to first browse through the career ideas that appear to be most interesting. Then check out the others—you never know what might interest you when you know more about it. As you read each profile, think about how well it matches up with what you learned about yourself in Section 1: **Discover You at Work**. Narrow down your options to a few careers and use the rating system

described below to evaluate your interest levels.

- **No way!** There's not even a remote chance that this career is a good fit for me. (Since half of figuring out what you do want to do in life involves figuring out what you don't want to do, this is not a bad place to be.)
- **This is intriguing**. I want to learn more about it and look at similar careers as well. (The activities outlined in Section 3: **Experiment with Success** will be especially useful in this regard.)
- **This is it!** It's the career I've been looking for all my life and I want to go after it with all I've got. (Head straight to Section 3: **Experiment with Success**.)

Governance

Governance includes all levels of elected and appointed officials who are responsible for making and executing public policy. This includes everyone from city mayors, county commissioners, and governors to senators, representatives, and the U.S. president. Those most likely to succeed in these types of careers possess exceptional leadership, consensus-building, and conflict resolution skills. Of course, getting enough votes to win an election is another critical factor. Governance careers profiled in this book include congressional aide, lobbyist, politician, and public attorney.

National Security

Keeping America safe is the number one priority for those working in national security occupations. At the top of the list of those serving in these often noble professions are the nation's municipal police officers and firefighters. At the national level this pathway includes those working for agencies such as the Federal Bureau of Investigation, Central Intelligence Agency, the Secret Service, the Bureau of Alcohol, Tobacco and Firearms.

This list would not be complete without including the 1.4 million men and women who serve in the nation's armed services—the Army, Air Force, Navy, Marines, and Coast Guard. National security professions profiled in this book include air marshal, air traffic controller, cryptographer, FBI special agent, firefighter, intelligence analyst, military serviceperson, park ranger, and police officer.

Foreign Service

Foreign service personnel represent American interests throughout the world in embassies, consulates, and other diplomatic missions. These professionals bring varied and often impressive expertise to areas as diverse as international law, world health, terrorism, and diplomacy. In addition to serving in the nation's capital, many foreign service professionals are assigned to overseas posts that include both modern democracies and third world countries. This book includes a profile about foreign service officers. In addition, public health official is another profile often associated with foreign service opportunities.

Planning

People involved in the planning occupations engage in a wide range of activities that share a common purpose of encouraging growth and revitalization in urban, suburban, and rural communities. They also help determine the best use of land for residential, institutional, and recreational purposes. Much of their work is devoted to helping local officials make informed decisions about social, economic, and environmental issues. Planning professions profiled in this book include conservationist, ecologist, economic development director, meteorologist, transportation manager, and urban planner.

A Note on Websites

Websites tend to move around a bit. If you have trouble finding a particular site, use an Internet browser to search for a specific website or type of information.

Revenue and Taxation

Among the most important government occupations are those associated with revenue and taxation. While no one particularly enjoys paying taxes, everyone appreciates the many benefits their tax dollars provide. People working in revenue and taxation professions are tasked with varied responsibilities associated with collecting taxes, reviewing tax returns, and conducting audits. Revenue and taxation careers profiled in this book include budget analyst and IRS agent.

Regulation

Regulatory professions generally require two types of expertise. First, most regulatory professionals are knowledgeable experts in a particular industry, the environment, or technology. Second, these same professionals must possess in-depth knowledge of the laws, rules, and regulatory systems associated with a given industry, the environment, or technology. They use this expertise to ensure the health and safety of our nation, its economy, and its environment. Regulatory professions profiled in this book include customs and border protection agent, election supervisor, food and drug scientist, and immigration agent.

Public Management and Administration

An estimated 8.6 million people work in the public sector in jobs associated with the business of running governments, nonprofit organizations, and charitable foundations. Various occupations in the pathway are associated with budgeting, personnel management, procurement, and other aspects of public management. Public management and administration careers profiled in this book include city manager, development director, emergency services coordinator, media relations specialist, postal service worker, public administrator, public policy advisor, and social worker.

As you explore the individual careers in this book and others in this series, remember to keep what you've learned about yourself in mind. Consider each option in light of what you know about your interests, strengths, work values, and work personality.

Pay close attention to the job requirements. Does it require math aptitude? Good writing skills? Ability to take things apart and visualize how they go back together? If you don't have the necessary abilities (or don't have a strong desire to acquire them), you probably won't enjoy the job.

In the following section, you'll find in-depth profiles about 35 careers representing the government and public service sectors. Some of these careers you may already know about. Others will present new ideas for your consideration. All are part of a dynamic and important segment of the U.S. economy.

find your air marshal future

air marshal

Next time you take a flight, observe the passengers closely. One could be a federal air marshal (FAM). Air marshals or sky marshals disguise themselves as ordinary passengers on flights that are considered high risk. Travelers should never know they are onboard unless an incident happens that threatens the safety of the passengers and crew. Since air marshals cannot be on all flights, they keep their assignments a secret to discourage hijackers.

If someone aboard the plane suddenly poses a threat, the marshal reacts instantly. To handle an in-flight emergency, marshals rely on quick reflexes and solid training. They have the authority to make arrests and they know how to physically restrain a person and, in extreme cases, use firearms.

The Federal Air Marshal Service dates back to 1968 when it was part of the Federal Aviation Administration's (FAA) Sky Marshal Program. The program employed 33 FAMs up until September 11, 2001. After terrorists struck that day, the federal government authorized an increase in hiring and in a few days received 200,000 applications. There is now an undisclosed number of air marshals protecting our air carriers, passengers, and crews. They are key members of the U.S. Department of Homeland Security and our country's war against terrorism.

Search It!
Federal Air Marshal Service at *www.ice.gov/graphics/fams*

Read It!
Inside ICE newsletter at *www.ice. gov/graphics/news/insideice/ index.htm*

Learn It!
● A bachelor's degree or three years' experience
● Completion of federal air marshal training program

Earn It!
Median annual salary is $60,150. (Source: U.S. Office of Personnel Management)

Find It!
Look into job openings at USAJOBS at *http://jobsearch. usajobs.opm.gov*. The site is called "your one-stop source for Federal jobs."

Get Started Now!

Secure a job as a federal air marshal by doing the following:

● Knowing about airline safety can help in this job. Check out the websites *www.airlinesafety.com* and *http://aviation-safety.net*.
● Physical fitness is vital so stay in shape.
● Ultimately, this law enforcement job may require you to subdue and restrain people. Any course you take today in self-defense, martial arts, or marksmanship could help.

Hire Yourself!

Before applying to be an air marshal, you need to hone your observational skills. Marshals need to be attuned to anything suspicious. To sharpen your "danger radar," your assignment is to make a complete tour of your school grounds noting anything that is potentially suspicious or dangerous—from people who look unfamiliar to bags that have been left unattended to doors that have been left open. Make a list of everything you see with notes on why these things are suspicious.

While they must be alert and check for suspicious travelers, marshals spend most of their time waiting. They should really enjoy traveling in planes because most of their work time is spent sitting in planes, eating those little bags of pretzels, and watching films on tiny screens. The work sometimes requires marshals to be away from families and friends a bit more than the average job. Assignments to foreign locations can take days or more than a week at a time to complete. Typically, though, they fly four to five hours a day and work 18 days a month.

Marshals cannot drink alcohol or sleep while on duty. They often work in pairs with one usually seated in the front of the plane and the other seated towards the rear. A large aircraft such as a Boeing 747 or Airbus 340 may require multiple pairs of FAMs.

Those applying for FAM positions must be under 40 years of age and undergo a tough training program that begins with seven weeks at the Federal Law Enforcement Training Center in Artesia, New Mexico. Here they learn constitutional law, basic marksmanship, physical fitness, defensive tactics, emergency medical skills, fundamental law enforcement, and investigative and administrative practices. If they pass the first phase of the training, candidates move on to the William J. Hughes Technical Center in Atlantic City, New Jersey, where they learn behavioral observation, strength conditioning, intimidation tactics, close-quarters self-defense techniques, and aircraft systems emergency procedures. FAMs must also prove extreme accuracy in handgun marksmanship.

Upon graduation from phase two of training, newly appointed federal air marshals are assigned to one of 21 field offices to begin flying missions. They must dress very neatly and follow military grooming, which some critics say makes them too conspicuous. Candidates for this job should be able to handle extremely stressful situations as well as long stretches with little activity. Top physical shape is essential.

air traffic controller

The air traffic control system is like a giant highway in the sky. Every day, pilots ferry passengers and cargo over crowded flight routes, much like cars and trucks navigate busy thoroughfares on the ground. But unlike routes on the ground, pilots have no lane lines to follow and no easy way to see if another plane is about to cross their path. How do pilots avoid collisions, navigate through fog and rough weather, and land safely at a jam-packed airport? They rely on the guidance of air traffic controllers. These professionals act as a pilot's right-hand assistant on the ground, directing planes and coordinating flight routes to assure safe and efficient air travel.

From their airport towers, the traffic controllers monitor every plane from take-off to touch-down, passing off tracking to different teams as

Get Started Now!

To set your career flight pattern as an air traffic controller, try the following:

- Take classes in English and speech to learn effective communication. Take classes in math, physics, and electronics, which will later help you understand the mechanics of flight.
- Play sports that require quick decision making, like soccer, basketball, or hockey. Even video games may be helpful in developing the ability to follow electronic images on a computer screen and make snap decisions.
- Inquire at your local airport if it might be possible to get a tour of the air traffic controller's tower. This may be more difficult nowadays for security reasons, but an in-person visit will give you a bird's eye view of the job.
- Visit *www.faa.gov/education* for games, exercises, and information about flying.

Search It!
Federal Aviation Administration (FAA) at *www.faa.gov*

Read It!
FAA Air Traffic Control Library at *www.faa.gov/atpubs*

Learn It!
- Three years of full-time work experience, four years of college, or a combination of both
- Successful completion of FAA-approved education program (find schools at *www.faa.gov/careers/employment/AT-CTI-MAP.htm*)

Earn It!
Median annual salary is $91,600. (Source: U.S. Department of Labor)

Find It!
Nearly all air traffic controllers work for the FAA, under the U.S. Department of Transportation. Look for job leads at USAJOBS, *www.usajobs.opm.gov*.

a plane progresses along its route. Before a plane even leaves the ground, pilots must file their flight plans with flight service station controllers. These workers are experts on the terrain, airports, and navigational facilities in their areas. By radio or computer, flight service station controllers give pilots pre-flight briefings on weather conditions, suggested routes and altitudes, indications of turbulence, and other flight safety information.

When a plane is ready to take off, airport tower controllers coordinate the order of planes leaving the airport to make sure they don't collide with each other or with people or vehicles on the tarmac. They normally direct air traffic only within 30 miles of an airport. When planes leave that airspace, an en route controller takes over. These controllers monitor air traffic between airports using radar and computers. They issue pilots in-flight instructions, clearance, and advice as planes pass through their jurisdiction. When a plane leaves the airspace assigned to an en route center, control passes to the next center or to a tower controller if the plane is ready to land.

Air traffic controllers typically work a standard 40-hour week in comfortable, air-conditioned towers. However, juggling multiple flight routes while communicating simultaneously with several pilots takes tremendous concentration and is often highly stressful. Air traffic controllers must stay calm in emergency situations and make quick decisions. Any hesitancy or errors could contribute to a disastrous air accident.

Virtually all air traffic controllers work for the Federal Aviation Administration (FAA), which has a rigorous set of qualifications for its applicants. Entry-level applicants must be no older than 30 and able to pass a physical exam and psychological test. Their vision must be corrected to 20/20 and they must be able to speak clearly. They also need to complete four years of college, gain three years of general work experience, or a combination of the two. If applicants meet all these criteria, they then must attend an FAA-approved education program, offered at

Hire Yourself!

Weather can be an important consideration for air traffic controllers. Winds, rain, and other bad weather conditions can influence whether planes are allowed to take off or not. Use the weather resources at *www.faa.gov/weather* to determine if current weather conditions are favorable for flights between airports in Los Angeles (LAX) and Boston (BOS); Dallas (DFW) and Seattle (SEA); and Atlanta (ATL) and Chicago (ORD). Make a chart to report your findings.

13 schools across the country. Applicants must score satisfactorily on a qualifying exam to be eligible to attend a 12-week FAA training academy. Upon graduation, they are finally placed in positions as air traffic controllers.

Air traffic controllers have very good job security and, even though fewer people travel during recessions, controllers are rarely laid off. If they continue to meet proficiency and medical requirements, air traffic controllers can earn relatively high pay and receive great benefits right up until mandatory retirement at age 56.

Search It!

The Association of
Government Accountants at
www.agacgfm.org

Read It!

Weekly on-line journal for accounting, finance, and banking at **www.
careerbank.com**

Learn It!

- Bachelor's degree in finance-
  related area of study
- Master's degree or CPA (Certi-
  fied Public Accountant) creden-
  tial for advancement

Earn It!

Median annual salary is $52,480.
(Source: U.S. Department of Labor)

Find It!

Budget analysts can look for government openings at **http://aga.
careerbank.com** or in the public
and private sector by searching
sites like **www.monster.com** or
www.careerbuilder.com.

find your budget analyst future

budget analyst

Cash flow is one thing that corporations large and small, government agencies, and nonprofit organizations all have in common: money comes in and money goes out. When Nike's product sales are up, money comes in. When citizens are taxed, money is received by the government. When a fund-raiser is successful, a nonprofit raises funds to work with. Now, the question is: what to do with this money? In order for any business entity to be successful it must distribute its resources in the most efficient way possible. This is why budget analysts are needed. Their primary responsibility is to develop an organization's budget and monitor how closely they follow it.

Budget analysts examine past spending trends and project future financial needs. Regardless of how much capital or how many resources a company has at its disposal, if it does not allocate them responsibly—even shrewdly—it puts itself at risk of bankruptcy. In private-sector firms, a budget analyst devises ways of distributing funds with the goal of increasing profits. In the public sector, an analyst's goal is more "performance-oriented," or getting more done with the available resources.

Budget analysts work on a budget cycle. At the beginning of each cycle, managers and directors give analysts projected costs for different

Get Started Now!

A career as a budget analyst may add up for you. Use these strategies to get ready:
- Analysts need exceptional quantitative and analytical skills—classes in statistics and economics will help.
- English and composition classes will develop crucial communication skills, which analysts rely on to explain results.
- If your school has a Junior Achievement club (**www.ja.org**), join it!

Hire Yourself

As class treasurer, you are responsible for coming up with the budget for the senior class trip to Disneyworld. Go on-line to find group rates for airfare, hotel accommodations, tickets for entertainment, and meals for a three-day visit. Report your findings in a spreadsheet using Microsoft Excel or another type of software program.

programs. These reports detail the expected costs for new and existing initiatives and operations. It is the job of the budget analyst to review these projections to make sure they are accurate and meet regulations both within and outside the company. They will perform cost-benefit analysis and consider spending alternatives where appropriate.

After reviewing budget proposals across departments, analysts will consolidate them and draw up summaries. The purpose of these summaries is to offer suggestions in favor of or against original budget requests. These summaries are given to upper management, where the final say on a budget rests.

If a government office is overspending, budget analysts may recommend ways to save money, such as layoffs. Or, alternately, they may suggest a redistribution of resources—perhaps moving employees from one office or department to another where productivity would be enhanced. Once a budget has been approved and implemented, analysts are responsible for seeing that it is followed. In situations where it is not, analysts consider the advantages or disadvantages of changing the budget and adjust the numbers accordingly.

Since budget analysts interact constantly with other employees and are responsible for drawing up budget reports, it is essential that they have excellent written and oral communication skills. They also need to be proficient in various computer software programs. Spreadsheet, database, and word processing programs, such as Microsoft Excel, Access, and Word, respectively, are used extensively. Financial and report writing software programs are also helpful.

Budget analysts generally work in office environments but sometimes travel to various locations in order to gather relevant data. Longer hours are not uncommon, especially during the beginning stages of budget development and during periods of budget review.

Analysts working for the government typically need a bachelor's degree, preferably in an area related to finance such as accounting, business, public administration, or economics. Those with a master's

degree have an edge in the job hunt and are the more likely candidates for promotions.

Opportunities for new analysts are expected to grow in the near future, but those entering the field must be prepared. Typically entry-level analysts with the federal government must complete specific training programs, while rookies at private-sector firms are either expected to hit the ground running or start by reviewing past budget trends or assisting more seasoned budget analysts.

find your city manager future

city manager

Behind every city, large or small, is a city manager working hard to keep it running smoothly. These professionals, called city managers, city administrators, or chief administrative officers (CAOs), are important decision-makers who influence the day-to-day operations of local governments at every level.

City mangers are the quintessential "movers and shakers" of municipal government and have a wide variety of responsibilities. They perform the same types of functions that a chief executive officer (CEO) performs for a business—responsible for keeping tabs on the overall effectiveness of each department and service rather than managing the nitty-gritty details of a particular department. They coordinate and manage the activities of all city departments and offices, prepare the city's annual budget, oversee the implementation of all city programs, and provide administrative assistance and support to the city council. City managers typically work out of an office in city hall and rely on the assistance of a variety of department heads, managers, and staff to keep everything on track. The size of the city determines the size of the support staff.

Ask any city manager and they are likely to agree that stress management is the number one skill necessary for success in their line of work. That's because crisis resolution is one of the most dependable

Get Started Now!

Get ready to storm city hall with the following ideas:
- Get involved in your school's student council or in a leadership capacity of a school or sports team.
- Ask a school guidance counselor or favorite teacher to help arrange a tour of your local city hall.
- Attend a meeting of your local city council to learn about issues currently facing your city.

Search It!
International City/County Management Association at *http://icma.org* and National Civic League at *www.ncl.org*

Read It!
Find links to a wide variety of resources by running a search using the keywords *municipal government* at the Questia Online Library at *www.questia.com*.

Learn It!
- Bachelor's degree in administration, commerce, finance, or public relations.
- Proficiency in both English and Spanish a plus

Earn It!
Average annual salary is $94,472. (Source: International City/County Management Association)

Find It!
Peruse job postings at the International City/County Management Association website at *http://jobs.icma.org*.

aspects of the job—whether it involves a broken water main or clearing the city's roadways after a winter blizzard.

Good people skills is another common asset found among successful city managers. The job involves direct contact with everyone from the mayor to the sanitation workers who collect the city's trash, which makes excellent and versatile communication skills absolutely essential.

Additional skill requirements include an educational background in administration, commerce, finance, or public relations. In many cases, proficiency in a second language such as Spanish is especially useful. Since city managers are generally appointed to their positions by a city's mayor, a certain degree of political networking often precedes their appointments. Once appointed, city managers work directly for the mayor, and like the mayor, answer to the city council.

According to the *Occupational Outlook Handbook*, employment prospects for those seeking careers in administrative services and facility management is expected to grow at an average pace. However, since by the very nature of the job there is only one city manager for every city, competition is keen and positions go to well-educated, experienced, and well-connected candidates.

WATER MAIN DAMAGED

NOTIFY POLICE
REROUTE TRAFFIC
DEPT HEAD STREET REPAIRS
REPAIR CREW

find your future
congressional aide

congressional aide

If you want to work for issues you believe in, and you tend to gravitate toward school subjects such as political science, economics, and history, then you might consider becoming a congressional aide. It's a job that puts you right at the heart of the political process. Congress is made up of a fascinating mix of people hailing from all parts of the country, and there's no better way to watch democracy in action than by participating in its day-to-day operations.

As you may remember from one of your government classes, Congress is made up of two branches: the Senate and the House of Representatives. Because members of Congress spend half the year in Washington, D.C., and the other half in their home state, they require a staff in each location. The D.C.-based committee staff concentrates on legislative work while the personal staff takes care of business, such as public relations and constituent inquiries, in the congressperson's home state.

Senators and representatives could not do their jobs without the help of their aides. Congressional aides handle much of the clerical work that keeps the legislative process moving: typing and filing, answering mail,

Search It!
The U.S. Senate at *www.senate.gov* and the House of Representatives at *www.house.gov*

Read It!
Find out how Congress really works at *www.YourCongress.com*

Learn It!
- Bachelor's degree in political science, pre-law, government affairs, or other liberal arts major
- Many colleges and universities offer congressional internship programs, or visit *www.studentjobs.gov* or *www.politixgroup.com/dcintern.htm* for more information

Earn It!
Median annual salary ranges between $23,000 and $28,000. (Source: The Politix Group)

Find It!
Search on-line job listings for Capitol Hill newspapers *Roll Call* (*www.rcjobs.com*) and *The Hill* (*www.hillnews.com/classifieds/employment.shtm*).

Get Started Now!
To make sure you're the best candidate for the job, you should:
- Take courses in political science, public speaking, economics, history, and English at school.
- Participate in student government, either by running for office yourself or by contributing to another person's campaign.
- Volunteer in a local election, such as a race for city council, in your hometown.

answering phones, transcribing reports, and participating in meetings. While the hours can be long and pay relatively low, working as an aide is a great entry into the world of politics. It provides a way to gain practical experience navigating the unpredictable currents of political life. Congressional aides may go on to become speech writers, press secretaries, or lobbyists. Even if you don't pursue a political career, "Hill experience" will put rocket boosters on your resume.

While most committee aides have an advanced degree—usually in law or journalism—personal aides require only a bachelor's degree. Congressional aides in the Senate generally earn more than those who work in the House. These positions can be highly competitive and many aides get hired as a result of personal connections, so it helps to know someone who works in Congress. Working as an intern can help you meet the right people.

find your future

conservationist

conservationist

From oil to lumber to fresh water, our earth's natural resources are in limited supply, yet we all depend on them for our everyday existence—for driving, for building homes, and, in the case of the nation's water supplies, to support our very existence. To make sure our precious natural resources are protected and managed wisely, the federal government employs conservationists. These professionals manage, develop, and safeguard a variety of natural areas on both land and sea. Regulating the use of nature can help protect our resources so they can be enjoyed by generations to come.

Most conservationists specialize in a particular area, such as wildlife management, range management, soil and water conservation, or forest management. Like other conservationists, foresters want to accommodate for the use of resources without over-harvesting. To estimate how many trees can be harvested, foresters weigh factors such as the number of adult trees, the amount of new planting, and the forest's growth pattern. To complete measurements on the trees, foresters rely on special

Get Started Now!

To start planning your career as a conservationist, do the following:

- Take courses in biology, math, and computer science to help understand natural resource availability and the tools for management.
- Join a group that promotes outdoors appreciation and survival skills, such as the Boy Scouts and Girl Scouts.
- Look into other environmental groups such as the Sierra Club (*www.sierraclub.org*) and the National Wildlife Federation (*www.nwf.org*).

Search It!
Society of American Foresters at *www.safnet.org*

Read It!
National Parks magazine at *www.npca.org/magazine*

Learn It!
A bachelor's degree in forestry, range management, or a related field is the minimum requirement for conservation jobs.

Earn It!
Median annual salary is $50,340. (Source: U.S. Department of Labor)

Find It!
About two-thirds of conservationists work for federal, state, or local government agencies. Look for job leads at the U.S. Forest Service (*www.fs.fed.us*).

Hire Yourself!

The local chapter of the Sierra Club has hired you to create a poster campaign to help educate the public about local environmental issues and concerns. For current information, start your research at the Sierra Club website (*www.sierraclub.org*), click on the "My Backyard" icon, and follow the instructions to access local information. Use your findings to create sketches of three posters proposing solutions for three prominent problems.

tools—clinometers to measure tree height, tapes to measure diameter, and increment borers and bark gauges that help estimate tree growth.

In the past few decades, foresters and other conservationists use high-tech tools to do their work, turning to computerized resources like Geographic Information Systems (GIS) and remote sensing (aerial photographs and other imagery taken from airplanes and satellites) to get a broad view of existing resources. Remote sensing and GIS can be used to create maps that help track resource use from year to year.

After taking into account the amount and current use of available resources, conservationists develop plans to sustain the natural resources. To decide on land use, conservationists may weigh the opinions of landowners, farmers, government officials, and the general public. Their plans must accommodate the changing, and often divergent, needs of humans and nature.

Some conservationists work in a laboratory or an office, but most spend a good portion of time working outside. The outdoor life requires that those interested in this career be physically hardy and nature lovers. Since they are often striving to balance competing interests—those who want to use our resources and those who want to save resources—conservationists must work well with people and have good communication and negotiation skills.

Additionally, the job requires at least a bachelor's degree in forestry, range management, or a similar discipline. Students in these programs mix general science courses like ecology, biology, or taxonomy (the classification of organisms in an ordered system) with more specialized studies such as forest inventory or wildlife habitat assessment. They also take plenty of computer science courses, where they learn how to use tools like remote sensing and GIS.

find your future
cryptographer

Search It!
National Security Agency (NSA) at
www.nsa.gov

Read It!
Find an introduction to cryptography
at ***www.cryptographyworld.com***

cryptographer

Do you love challenging yourself with brain-busting puzzles? Is solving complicated math problems your idea of fun? Do the words "secret decoder ring" boost your heart rate? If so, you might think about becoming a FROPQNKRVPXJR—that's a code for CRYPTOGRAPHER, also known as a cryptanalyst, cipher expert, or secret code writer. The science of cryptography, from the Greek for "hidden writing," currently deals mostly with encryption, decryption, and authentication. Encryption is the transformation of data into a form that can only be read by someone with the necessary knowledge or key. Decryption is the transformation of that data back into a readable form. Authentication ensures that only the person for whom that information is intended gains access to it.

Learn It!
● College degree with almost any major
● Successful completion of the National Security Agency's Cryptanalysis Intern Program (***http://www.nsa.gov/careers/ careers_8.cfm***)

Earn It!
Average entry level salary is $34,184.
(Source: National Security Agency)

Get Started Now!

If you're looking to break into the field of cryptography, here are some ways to prepare:

● Take advanced math classes and courses in computer programming, which provide a useful background for future cryptographers.
● Hone your code-cracking skills by solving cryptopuzzles—check out some of the many websites and on-line magazines that feature cryptograms and other code puzzles for you to twist your brain around, such as ***www.allstarpuzzles.com*** and ***www.crpuzzles.com***.
● Balance your technological training with literary studies and other courses in the humanities. Cryptographers need to think both critically and creatively. Excellent writing and communication skills will make you a stronger candidate for this job.

Find It!
Find out about opportunities for cryptographers at the National Security Agency website at ***www.nsa.gov/careers*** and employment opportunities in the Armed Forces at ***www. todaysmilitary.com***.

Cryptographers function like digital locksmiths. They help keep electronic information safe by devising ways to encrypt and decrypt it. In the private sector, cryptographers work to keep Internet communications secure. Electronic banking, bar codes, and cellular phone service all rely on cryptography. The U.S. government needs code makers and code breakers to make sure that sensitive military and government data stays secret, especially now that terrorism is an overwhelming national concern. Cryptographers help combat terrorism by creating codes to protect classified information, working to identify the weaknesses in existing data systems, and gathering knowledge about other countries' communications.

To stay ahead of the hackers, cryptographers need to master cutting-edge computer technologies in a rapidly evolving field. Yet this up-to-the-minute profession has a long and fascinating history. Julius Caesar supposedly created one of the first cryptographic systems to send secret instructions to his Roman generals on the battlefield. The history of cryptography also includes the coded information stitched into quilts by African-American slaves and the use of Native American code talkers during World War II, who safely passed messages in the Navaho language that the enemy never deciphered. Modern computer science actually has its roots in the ancient science of cryptography.

Today, cryptographers usually have backgrounds in mathematics, but the field is not limited to math majors or individuals with prior experience in computer programming. The National Security Agency (NSA), the main government employer in this field, hires people with both technical and seemingly unrelated degrees such as in music and history. More important than technical experience is the ability to work on extremely challenging problems. Would-be cryptographers should have strong critical thinking skills. Excellent communication skills and fluency in other languages may also count in your favor.

While government jobs for cryptographers tend to be concentrated on the East Coast in Washington, D.C., cipher experts may be based in other sections of the country or even overseas. Due to the sensitive nature of this work and its importance to national security, applicants and members of their immediate families must be U.S. citizens. Aspiring cryptographers have to submit to a rigorous background check and pass a polygraph exam. Applicants must be granted a security clearance, which means they can be trusted to handle classified information, before they are hired. With national security a top priority, employment prospects for cryptographers are strong.

find your future
customs and border protection officer

customs and border protection officer

When you return from a trip overseas, sometimes you bring back more than memories of the exotic places and unusual foods. You might bring back jewelry or clothing, for instance. If these are items you have to "declare," you may have to pay a visit to a customs and border protection officer at the airport. Customs officers are responsible for maintaining the flow of legitimate trade and travel into and out of the United

Get Started Now!

Use these strategies to get ready for a future as a customs agent:

● Fluency in a foreign language, especially Spanish, will help.
● Classes in history and geography are beneficial as well to help you understand other cultures and products that may be imported from different regions.
● With a great deal of information technology being implemented in this line of work, it pays to be computer-literate. It may help to take a programming class, or simply stay up-to-date with the latest computer software.
● Customs work is very much like police work. A career shadowing day or internship with your local police precinct can give you a taste of the type of work that might be involved. Also, look into the CBP's Law Enforcement Explorer program at *www.customs.gov*. The program lets young people assist with passenger processing, observe surveillance operations and vessel searches, and more.

Hire Yourself

You've just been hired as a customs officer. Go on-line and find Internet resources related to the Trade Act of 2002. A useful place to start your research is this U.S. Department of Labor webpage: *www.doleta.gov/tradeact/ 2002act_directives.cfm*. You'll also find a summary from the Robert Wood Johnson Foundation at this Web address: *www.statecoverage.net/pdf/issuebrief303trade.pdf*. Prepare a briefing paper outlining the key points of the Act.

States. They safeguard our country at ports of entry, from air, land, and sea. They make sure nothing harmful crosses our borders, and nothing is taken from a country without authority or proper compensation. Officers look for smuggled drugs, merchandise on which taxes must be charged, and personal documents that may not be in order.

As part of the U.S. Department of Homeland Security, customs and border protection officers are law enforcement officers. They often wear badges and carry firearms, batons, and handcuffs. They examine cargo, baggage, and items worn or carried onto a car, ship, train, or plane traveling into or out of the United States. In order to do this, they may have to inspect, count, weigh, or in some manner, measure, the contents of a person's belongings. They may have to cut or pry into potential hiding places using power tools. Sometimes, they pat down suspects in the search for contraband or they may use dogs to sniff out illegal drugs or explosive materials. They often collect duties, or monetary fees, for some items being transported. Upon locating illicit items, agents seize the property and the perpetrator and hold them until they are relayed to the proper authorities.

Customs and border protection officers also screen potentially harmful food and agricultural shipments such as beef products that may have mad cow disease and plants that may have crop-destroying insects. They are also trained to look for specific items that may cause bio- and agro-terrorism. If contaminants enter the country, disease and infection could result. Officers work with the Food and Drug Administration (FDA) to make sure proper procedures are followed to properly dispose of or contain such materials.

Customs and border protection professionals rely on some of the most sophisticated technology in the world to protect our ports of entry. Automated Targeting Systems (ATS) and the Automated Export Systems (AES) obtain information that could help pinpoint a threat before it reaches our borders. X-ray machines and radiation-technology devices detect hazardous or illegal materials. New surveillance intelligence systems are able to monitor borders with specialized sensors and night-day cameras.

Most customs officers work full time with shifts of officers on duty around the clock, every day of the year. In some instances they call in experts to assist in unusual customs situations. Such an expert might be used to analyze and authenticate artwork or archaeological artifacts. In these extreme cases, agents consult their legal department, and often items are seized, held, and repatriated to their rightful owners.

In order to become a customs officer, you must first be a U.S. citizen and have a valid U.S. driver's license. At the time of appointment, you must be between the ages of 20 and 37. You must have at least a bachelor's degree and three years of general work experience. Higher level positions require one year of specialized experience, sometimes require advanced educational degrees, and may involve passing more rigorous background checks, drug tests, and medical and fitness examinations. Once hired, officers must complete a rigorous 12-week training program at the U.S. Customs and Border Protection Academy in Glynco, Georgia.

Officers must meet many physical demands as well as psychological ones—they are, after all, responsible for locating contraband and arresting those carrying it. Officers need a no-nonsense demeanor and should be trained in questioning techniques to get information from suspects. In some instances, suspects can get violent or try to flee, so officers must be prepared to respond appropriately in these potentially dangerous situations. They must be very alert at all times, keeping a close watch of surveillance cameras and other monitors.

Although the job is very demanding and the CBP hires only very motivated, highly trained individuals, competition to enter this field is strong. Those who enter the field often take great pride in defending their country.

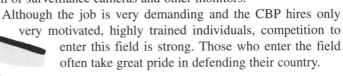

find
development
your director
future

development director

Were you the kid who went door to door raising money for the American Heart Association or other organizations? If so, then you might consider becoming a development director for a nonprofit firm. Legally speaking, the term "nonprofit" designates any organization granted a tax-exempt status by the Internal Revenue Service (IRS). Nonprofits range from arts and cultural organizations such as museums and symphonies, to private colleges and universities, to hospitals, to faith-based organizations such as the Salvation Army. Some nonprofit organizations employ thousands of workers while others are run by just a handful of volunteers. Since nonprofits rely on the generous contributions of individuals, businesses, and foundations for financial support, nonprofits are always looking for talented communicators and organizers with proven fund-raising skills. A development director needs all of these skills—and more.

Get Started Now!

Here are the steps you can take now toward a career in this field:

- Get fund-raising experience by volunteering at a local nonprofit. Volunteer experience can have the same impact as professional fund-raising experience on your resume.
- Take courses in nonprofit management at a local college, university, or business school.
- Identify nonprofits where you might like to work and go on-line to learn as much as you can about the core values and mission of each organization.

Search It!
Action Without Borders at *www.idealist.org*

Read It!
Chronicle of Philanthropy at *www.philanthropy.com*

Learn It!
A bachelor's degree is required but, to advance, many professionals earn a master's in philanthropic studies or nonprofit management.

Earn it!
Average annual salary is $55,569. (Source: Association for Volunteer Administration)

Find It!
Many useful websites specialize in nonprofit job listings such as *www.nonprofits.org* and *www.opportunityknocks.org*.

A development director's principal job is to oversee the fund-raising for a nonprofit organization. However, she or he may also be expected to write grants, identify and cultivate prospective donors, develop strategies for meeting funding goals, recruit and train volunteer fund-raisers, and manage development personnel. The development director reports directly to the firm's executive director, the CEO of a nonprofit organization.

Seven percent of the total U.S. workforce is employed by nonprofits. Ninety percent of these organizations are community-based organizations, or CBOs, which operate at the local rather than national level. Nonprofit firms are often family-friendly, offering workers more vacation time and more flexible schedules than for-profit companies. The proliferation of nonprofits means you can choose to work for an organization that shares your interests and concerns.

Just think how great it must feel to know that your efforts have helped to alleviate homelessness, brought relief to flood victims, or protected an endangered species. But however passionate you may be about "making a difference," you will not get very far in the nonprofit world without a good education and the skills and temperament most valued in this sector. Successful candidates for the position of development director have a bachelor's (and sometimes a graduate degree) and several years of proven success at fund-raising. (Luckily, volunteer opportunities to learn this skill abound.) Nonprofits look for candidates with technological savvy and experience with fund-raising software, as more of the work they do becomes computerized. In today's employment climate, good development directors are highly sought after. As government programs scale back and federal funds are less available, the ability to raise funds effectively becomes even more critical than ever for nonprofit organizations.

find your ecologist future

ecologist

To an ecologist, life on earth is like one giant jigsaw puzzle where land, water, trees, plants, animals, and people are all interconnected. Their job is to study how all the pieces fit together and to figure out better ways for all ecosystems to coexist.

Ecology is essentially a blend of all life sciences—including biology, geography, botany, and oceanography. Ecologists tend to specialize in one of three areas: biological ecology, physical ecology, and human ecology. Biological ecologists focus their efforts on issues related to wildlife, wetlands, marine life, and botany. Physical ecologists focus on soil science, meteorology, and geology. Human ecologists explore socioeconomic issues and ecological anthropology.

An area of particular concern to all ecologists is pollution. As protectors of the earth, they study the harmful effects that man has had on air, water, ground, plants, and animals. They look for ways to prevent further pollution and reverse the damage already done. These scientists grapple with environmental issues such as climate change, ozone depletion, species extinction, acid rain, and oil spills. An ecologist studying the diminishing wetlands may conduct research to determine why these lands are being drained and what can be done to slow the process or repair the damage. Another ecologist might study the effects of toxic

Search It!
The Ecological Society of America at *www.esa.org*

Read It!
Ecological and environmental news at the Natural Resources Defense Council at *www.nrdc.org*

Learn It!
● Bachelor's degree in environmental science or ecology
● Master's degree or doctorate often required for independent research and university positions

Earn It!
Median annual salary is $65,207. (Source: U.S. Department of Labor)

Find It!
Ecologists can look for positions within the federal government at the U.S. Office of Personnel Management (OPM) website at *www.usajobs.opm.gov*.

Get Started Now!

Use these strategies to get ready for a future as an ecologist:

● Math and science classes are essential—specifically, biology, chemistry, and statistics.
● Consider volunteering at a local park or wildlife reserve. You can also search for internships at *www.studentjobs.gov*.
● Learn about ecological causes and volunteer with groups such as the Sierra Club (*www.sierraclub.org*) and the Environmental Defense Fund (*www.edf.org*).

dumping on the population of frogs in a given area. Other scientists look into ways to improve existing resources, investigating ways to increase crop production, for example.

This type of work is sometimes conducted outdoors, where field research may involve anything from accessing damage from a forest fire to calculating the impact of snowmobile usage in a national park or even investigating a hazardous waste dump site. However, it is also common to find ecologists in a lab working at computers. Data crunching is a huge part of the job—using scientific and mathematical models to analyze relationships of actions and effects on the environment.

Ecologists work in both the public and private sectors. Some teach and conduct research through colleges and universities. Others start consulting firms where they may seek out government research contracts or conduct impact studies, while still others may work for companies that develop environmental services or products. The U.S. Department of the Interior is an example of a government agency that hires many ecologists. This federal agency manages many of our country's natural resources and is responsible for protecting wildlife and developing the nation's conservation policies.

Jobs in the field are expected to grow in the coming years and almost half of ecologists can expect to find jobs with the government. Building a career around ecology can be a good choice for those who are scientifically minded and want to help make the world a better place.

find
economic development
your director
future

economic development director

Imagine a town whose main economic attraction is a gold mine. When the mine is no longer productive, jobs dry up and many people are forced to leave. Eventually, schools and other services would close, and before you know it the town is completely abandoned. This scenario played out again and again back in the days of the Gold Rush. These towns exist today only as memories or as abandoned ghost towns.

Economic development directors work to save their cities from similar fates. Their job is to keep cities strong by creating jobs, attracting money, and improving the general quality of life. To achieve their goals, these professionals must be expert at finance, marketing, real estate development, education, public relations, transportation, and tax laws, among other things.

The key to economic development is jobs. In order to have jobs, economic developers make sure that zoning regulations and tax incentives are attractive for companies to move to the area or to expand their existing facilities. Quality of life is a critical factor influencing where a company

Search It!
National Congress for Community Economic Development at *www.ncced.org* and International Economic Development Council (IEDC) at *www.iedconline.org*

Read It!
Peruse the "Tools of the Trade" section of U.S. Department of Commerce website at *www.eda.gov*.

Learn It!
● Bachelor's degree in business administration, marketing, or economics
● Master's degree and business experience a plus

Earn It!
Typical earnings of economic development directors range between $50,000 and $100,000. (Source: IEDC)

Find It!
Find job postings at IEDC (*www.iedconline.org*) and of regional economic development associations (*www.eda.gov/Resources/StateLinks.xml*).

Get Started Now!
● Take courses that hone your skills in writing and public speaking.
● Learn about what is happening to support the economic development of your city, state, or region. Use the Internet to search for local economic development councils or associations.
● Find out if your school sponsors Young Entrepreneurs (*www.yeo.org*) or Junior Achievement (*www.ja.org*) organizations and get involved.

decides to operate. Ensuring that a city has good schools, affordable housing, museums and cultural facilities, a lively downtown area, and a low crime rate is another aspect of an economic development director's job.

However, even the most perfect city will not attract new business if no one knows about it. Getting the word out about a city's finer points is another function of the economic development director's job. This process is called marketing and it can take many forms—from mounting a general public relations campaign to designing a website or creating brochures and advertisements. It may involve visiting companies in targeted industries or attending trade shows. It may also involve positioning the city as a tourist destination and working to attract business conventions.

Finally, the economic development professional must work with local and state government and with community organizations to ensure that the business climate remains attractive. He or she may have to lobby politicians to improve local transportation, to approve tax cuts for new businesses, and to improve the schools and other quality of life factors.

Achieving these tasks requires a strong background in business. Successful economic development directors are excellent managers, organizers, communicators, and financial analysts. Many organizations, including the National Congress for Community Economic Development (at *www.ncced.org*) and the International Economic Development Council (at *www.iedconline.org*), offer professional development courses for people working in the field.

find your election supervisor future

election supervisor

In the words of Buddy Johnson, election supervisor for Florida's Hillsborough County, the ultimate role of an election supervisor is "create competent, confident voters in an atmosphere where everyone is treated with dignity and respect." According to his county's website this is accomplished by a relentless focus on "conducting flawless elections, removing any obstacle to voting, empowering voters through knowledge and continuously improving voting systems and technology. "

Unbeknownst to many voters is the fact that election supervisors work full time, all the time, and not just in election years. While an important part of their job is to conduct public elections for all levels of government—including city, state, and federal elections—in between elections they stay extremely busy with tasks that range from registering voters, issuing voter registration cards, and updating voter registration information to collecting financial disclosure reports from elected officials, compiling statistics on election results, and maintaining election equipment. They are also responsible for hiring and training poll workers and acquiring and equipping polling places. Another important responsibility involves verifying petitions for ballot initiatives and candidate qualifying

Get Started Now!

Cast your vote for a career as an election supervisor by:
- Helping run a friend's campaign for homecoming court or student council.
- Volunteering to work the polls during a local or national election. Some states require that workers be at least 17 years of age. Contact your local board of elections for information.
- Taking a course in statistics to enhance your number-crunching abilities.

Search It!
National Association of State Election Directors at *www.nased.org* and Election Assistance Commission at *www.eac.gov*

Read It!
Read the Help America Vote Act of 2002 at *www.fec.gov/hava/hava.htm*

Learn It!
- Many election officials have a law degree or at least a bachelor's degree in public administration
- Actual requirements vary from state to state

Earn It!
Annual salaries for government chief executives and legislators range between $11,460 and $81,230.
(Source: U.S. Department of Labor)

Find It!
Click on the tab for "Job Openings" at the Election Center website (*www.electioncenter.org*) for information about currently available positions in this field.

petitions. The bottom line is that their job is to protect every U.S. citizen's right to vote and to ensure that fair elections take place.

Most election officials work in offices housed in city or county government buildings. They typically work regular eight-hour business days except during the heat of an election when a good deal of overtime is common. Regardless of the size of the city or county they work for, all election supervisors are required to be nonpartisan and must refrain from absolutely any show of political favoritism.

Since, in a very literal sense, democracy depends on the work conducted by election supervisors; these government employees must approach each responsibility with diligence and an utmost attention to accuracy. Their success is judged by how well they safeguard our national creed that "every vote counts."

BALLOT

VOTE

find your
emergency services coordinator
future

emergency services coordinator

When the Congressional Act of 1803 was passed, organized federal emergency assistance was born. The act provided federal relief to a New Hampshire town that had been devastated by a massive fire. By 1979, several national disaster recovery and prevention plans existed to cover floods, hurricanes, earthquakes, and other types of major emergency situations. That same year, President Jimmy Carter merged these separate efforts to form the Federal Emergency Management Agency (FEMA). Today, emergency services coordinators are employed by the government to assist when an emergency—natural and otherwise—disrupts life in our communities. Beyond natural disasters, FEMA employees plan for potential emergencies associated with nuclear power plants, military chemical stockpile sites, or terrorist attacks.

Fortunately for those affected by all manner of catastrophe, relief efforts start long before disaster strikes. These professionals do not simply help a community recover from disaster; they attempt to mitigate

Get Started Now!

Use these strategies to get ready for a future as an emergency services coordinator:

- Classes in psychology and science will come in handy.
- Get involved in community service. You can practice helping people through an organized effort, such as a homeless shelter, public health center, or Habitat for Humanity.
- Take courses in first aid and CPR at a local hospital or a local Red Cross chapter.

Search It!
The Federal Emergency Management Agency (FEMA) at *www.fema.gov*

Read It!
FEMA news and press releases at *www.fema.gov/news/ recentnews.fema*

Learn It!
- High school diploma or equivalent
- Bachelor's degree or higher, depending on position

Earn It!
Median annual salary is $32,158. (Source: U.S. Department of Labor)

Find It!
Those interested in a position as an emergency services coordinator can find out more at *www.fema. gov/career*, or by visiting *www. usajobs.gov*.

emergencies—meaning they take action before anything has happened, in order to reduce the risk of loss. For example, they may survey land to ensure people are building safely within a floodplain, deliver sandbags to lessen flood damage, or provide insurance against emergencies not typically covered by private insurance companies (such as a flood).

Emergency services coordinators also work with media, law enforcement, school officials and other emergency personnel to keep the public aware and prepared for a disaster. This may mean consulting with the National Weather Service to update a community on the status of a hurricane in Florida, or working to make sure teachers in Oklahoma have adequate tornado protection plans.

Once a hurricane or a tornado has struck, the governor of the affected state must request a declaration of emergency by the U.S. president. A preliminary damage assessment (PDA) is conducted by state and local officials to help the president determine whether or not the affected region should be considered a disaster area.

After an emergency has been declared, FEMA workers get to work assessing damage, processing loans or grants to homeowners whose homes have been destroyed, providing legal assistance or crisis counseling to victims, and surveying land and structures to determine whether or not more long-term actions should be taken to reduce risk in the future.

Training and qualifications vary according to the type of work required for specific positions. For example, a FEMA budget analyst should have a degree related to finance or accounting, whereas a degree in architecture would be more appropriate for someone evaluating the risk of damage to a building. Specific education requirements are detailed in job descriptions on the FEMA website (*www.fema.gov*). In addition, applicants must complete courses via the Emergency Management Institute, as required for specific jobs. Applicants must be

Hire Yourself

You've just been hired by FEMA to work in an area prone to flooding. Your job is to provide information educating residents about what to do in the event of a major flood. Prepare a pamphlet of information to give to them. Use the resources provided on-line at *www.fema.gov/ library/prepandprev.shtm#floodhazard* to research this problem. The pamphlet should include ideas to prevent property damage, an emergency planning checklist, and survival tips.

U.S. citizens and must pass a drug test. Most workers must also be on-call 24 hours a day and be willing to work off-site, wherever disaster happens to strike.

Emergency relief can be high-stress and psychologically challenging. These professionals, after all, often dealing with people whose lives have been turned upside-down. Their communities, homes, life savings, or loved ones may have been taken from them in the blink of an eye. The work has its rewards though as it involves helping people recover from what is often the worst experience of their lives.

find your FBI special agent future

Search It!
The Federal Bureau of Investigation at *www.fbi.gov*

Read It!
The FBI's *Law Enforcement Bulletin* at *www.fbi.gov*

Learn It!
- Four-year degree from accredited college or university
- Three years' full-time work experience
- Fluency in a second language especially useful

Earn It!
Entry-level annual salary including law enforcement availability pay (LEAP) is $48,890.
(Source: U.S. Department of Labor)

Find It!
Those interested in a position with the FBI can apply on-line at *www.fbijobs.com* or through the mail.

FBI special agent

As stated in its mission, the sole purpose of the Federal Bureau of Investigation (FBI) is "to protect and defend the United States against terrorist and foreign intelligence threats and to enforce the criminal laws of the United States." Fulfilling this mission requires a dauntless cadre of agents working in every corner of the nation doing everything necessary to uphold federal laws. The work involves surveillance, transcription, research, coordination with local authorities, and report-writing. Agents may set up wire-taps to monitor phone calls, comb through business records, and track the movement of stolen property.

FBI agents actually have limited power to arrest perpetrators—an action usually performed by other law enforcement officers. FBI responsibilities inhabit a middle ground between the law enforcement efforts of local and state-level police and the special international operations of the Central Intelligence Agency (CIA).

The FBI is responsible for investigating violations in more than 200 categories of federal law. Some of these categories include counterter-

Get Started Now!

Use these strategies to get ready for a future as an FBI agent:

- Candidates need exceptional skills for analyzing both people and data. Psychology, math, and science classes are good preparation for this line of work, as well as biology, anthropology, chemistry, and molecular biology.
- The FBI has an internship program for undergraduate and graduate students only. Check out the requirements for participation on-line at *www.fbijobs.com/intern.asp*.
- The FBI website also offers fascinating information for students who are interested in the field. Profiles of FBI agents and their cases are presented at *www.fbi.gov/kids*.

rorism (efforts to fight terrorist cells), cyber crimes (such as hacking into computers to steal electronic information), public corruption (crimes within the government), organized crime (large criminal operations, such as the Mafia and gangs), and counterintelligence (preventing the penetration of U.S. intelligence or, to put it another way, tracking spies). They also handle crimes of copyright infringement, kidnapping, extortion, and drug trafficking.

There are many qualifications for becoming an agent. First, potential agents must be a U.S. citizen. They must also be between the ages of 23 and 37, and possess at least a bachelor's degree. It doesn't really matter what field of study the degree is in, so long as it has allowed the candidate to hone his or her research and analytical skills. That said, those with a degree in law or accounting have a slight edge, since a firm understanding of the law is, of course, a necessary prerequisite for someone whose job it is to investigate violations of that law. Accounting is another advantageous field of study because the FBI deals heavily in tracing finances and tracking complex account records. FBI accountants may often be called to testify in such cases. Those with a fluency in Arabic, Farsi, Pashto, Urdu, Chinese, Japanese, Korean, Russian, Spanish, or Vietnamese are especially attractive candidates.

In addition to these requirements, candidates must also pass stringent physical exams and extensive background checks. For example, one physical test is the "shuttle run," in which an applicant runs zigzagging through a series of cones as fast as he or she can. For the background checks, recruiters contact everyone from teachers and former employers to neighbors, doctors, and landlords. Candidates must pass a drug test and, in some cases, a polygraph (lie detector) test.

If a candidate passes muster, he or she spends four months at the FBI Academy in Quantico, Virginia, for training. The program comprises 708 instructional hours in academics, physical training/defensive tactics, and practical exercises. This training includes instructions in using firearms, handling a gun, and practicing on a shooting range. After this

program has been successfully completed, the recruit is placed in a field office. FBI agents must be willing to travel for particular assignments or relocate for new positions within the agency.

Despite all the challenges of the job, competition to get a position as an FBI agent is stiff. Salaries and benefits are attractive and the work can be varied and very rewarding.

firefighter

firefighter The shrill whine of a fire engine siren may conjure up images of a ladder and hose stretching up a tall apartment building in flames, or frantic residents fleeing from a raging forest fire. But as you pull your car aside to let a shiny fire engine speed past, the firefighters inside may be headed to any one of a number of emergencies. Firefighters not only attack possibly devastating fires, but they often also act as first responders for traffic accidents, medical emergencies, and other disasters. These everyday heroes risk their own lives to rescue others, including people, pets, and property.

Firefighters can work in a variety of environments, such as chemical plants, airports, and in neighborhood fire stations. These locations often require special types of training. For example, a firefighter who works at an outpost near Montana parklands will be skilled in fighting forest fires. Those who work in airports will know how to handle emergency aircraft landings.

Some days can be uneventful as firefighters spend much of their time on call at the firehouse, which usually looks like a specially equipped dormitory. They pass the time between alarms sleeping, eating communal meals, cleaning and maintaining equipment, and performing practice drills.

Search It!
International Association of
Firefighters at *www.iaff.org*

Read It!
Fire Engineering magazine at
http://fe.pennnet.com

Learn It!
- All firefighters have at least a high school diploma or general equivalency diploma (GED), but many have degrees from community colleges or universities in fire engineering or fire science
- New firefighters attend training courses at their department's training center or academy

Earn It!
Median annual salary is $38,280.
(Source: U.S. Department of Labor)

Find It!
Look for job leads at Firefighter Jobs, *www.firefighter-jobs. com*.

Get Started Now!

To get a jump on your career as a firefighter, do the following:
- Take classes in physics and engineering to get an understanding of how fires behave and spread.
- Take a course in sports medicine or first aid offered through your school or local Red Cross.
- Play sports like soccer or basketball to learn a sense of teamwork and stay in shape.

However, when an alarm sounds, firefighters drop whatever they're doing, slip on protective suits and equipment, and pile into their fire engine. Since every second counts, they race to the scene of the blaze as quickly and safely as possible. There, they work as a team under the direction of a superior officer, who develops a strategy for attacking each individual fire. Firefighters connect hoses to hydrants and switch on a pump that pushes water into high pressure hoses. They position ladders to help deliver water to where it's needed most, and they enter buildings to search for victims or valuable property. The job requires split-second decision making and intelligent strategizing to decide how to best contain and eliminate the fire.

Often people or animals will be trapped inside a burning structure, and rescuers must quickly decide on how to reach them (sometimes chopping through walls or ceilings with an axe) and bring them to safety. Once out of the fire, rescuers administer medical treatment and work with other emergency service providers, such as paramedics, to speed victims to hospitals. Because most firefighters are trained as emergency medical technicians, they are often called to respond to other emergencies, such as car accidents.

While a week or more may pass without a single alarm, sometimes multiple fires break out in a single day. To keep fresh, firefighters work on a shift basis—on duty for 24 hours, then off for 48 hours, with an extra day off at regular intervals. While subduing each blaze, firefighters face constant risk of injury or death from sudden cave-ins of floors, collapsing walls, and exposure to flames and toxic smoke. Layers of protective clothing and equipment such as oxygen masks can help ease some of these dangers, but there is no getting around the fact that this is a risky business.

Beyond mental alertness, firefighters must have good self-discipline, courage, endurance, and strength. Mechanical aptitude can help firefighters craft a plan of action and initiative, and good judgment is important for making decisions in the heat of the moment. Firefighters respond to each emergency as a team so they must also be able to work well with other people and take directions effectively.

Applicants for entry-level firefighting positions usually have to pass a written exam and tests of strength, physical stamina, coordination, and agility. They also have to pass a medical exam that includes a drug test. All firefighters must have at least a high school diploma or GED, but classes at a community college or university can help get applicants into competitive departments. After they have been recruited to a particular department, firefighters generally attend several weeks of training at their department's training center or academy. There, they learn the basics of firefighting through classroom instruction and practical training. After a firefighter has gained some experience on the job, some departments will offer tuition assistance or reimbursement for employees who want to go back to school or a two- or four-year degree in fire engineering or science. Openings for firefighter positions are often highly competitive. Although the job is dangerous and stressful, large numbers of applicants are drawn to the challenge and an opportunity to perform an important public service. Firefighting is an essential service, so firefighters are rarely laid off during budget cuts.

Search It!
Food and Drug Administration at
www.fda.org

Read It!
FDA Consumer Magazine at
www.fda.gov/fdac

Learn It!
A minimum of a bachelor's degree in the physical sciences, life sciences, or engineering.

Earn It!
Median annual salary is $55,904. (Source: U.S. Office of Personnel Management)

Find It!
Look at the employment possibilities by visiting FDA Employment at *www.fda.gov/jobs* or visit the federal government's employment information system at *www. USAJOBS.opm.gov*.

find
food and drug
your scientist
future

food and drug
scientist

If any part of the federal government could be considered "nurturing," it would have to be the Food and Drug Administration (FDA). This may seem like a stretch, but this agency, which is part of the U.S. Department of Health and Human Services, is dedicated to protecting the health and welfare of you, the American consumer. The FDA wants to make sure you're eating right—they set the standards for the labels you see on foods spelling out the nutritional content. FDA scientists want your food to be free of contaminants, like disease-causing organisms and chemicals, and it issues guidelines on food safety that can prevent food poisoning and other illness. The FDA doesn't want you to hurt yourself—it recently issued a warning to consumers about the risk of permanent eye injury, and even blindness, associated with decorative contact lenses. The agency is also taking a closer look at complications that can result from tattoos and breast implants.

These are just a few of the topics FDA scientists are working on. But, no matter what the area, they all evaluate consumer products, weighing

Get Started Now!
Start your research on a career as an FDA scientist:
- Build your educational background taking courses in biology, chemistry, physics, and calculus.
- Immerse yourself in science-related websites. Check out *http://sciencemaster.com*, *www.funsci.com*, and *www.brainpop.com*.
- A student job with the FDA can give a real feel for the work. Investigate the Student Educational Employment Program at *www.opm.gov/employ/students*.

Hire Yourself!

To get a summer job with the FDA, they want to see if you can read and interpret the nutrition facts printed on most packaged foods. Pick out three foods and compare the nutritional content. Which one has the most fat? Which one has the most cholesterol? Which one has the most sodium? Which one has the most carbohydrates? Which one has the most protein? Make a chart comparing the three products and put a big star by the one you determine to have the most nutritional value.

the risks against the benefits. Generally, their work falls into these different categories:

New product review. The FDA reviews the results from laboratory, animal, and clinical testing done by drug and cosmetic companies to determine if the products they want to put on the market are safe and effective. However, the FDA does not develop and test products itself. The agency also establishes standards and regulations for all medical devices from simple tongue depressors to pacemakers.

Keeping watch. The FDA keeps track of how products are manufactured and responds to reports of problems or newly identified risks. The FDA issues alerts and recalls on food items that can cause allergies or sickness. For instance, when a type of Halloween candy containing a certain egg protein was put on the market, the FDA issued a warning that it might cause an allergic reaction. The FDA checks shipments of imported products, and collects and tests samples for contamination. Scientific techniques for testing foods have come a long way from the early 1900s when the FDA employed a "poison squad," a group of people who were fed new food additives to test their safety.

Research. The FDA does research to provide scientific basis for its regulatory decisions. The agency uses its research results to set standards. Scientists are always looking to develop new test methods and ways to monitor products and study emerging risks. The FDA has studied the potential health problems associated with wireless phones, X rays, and microwaves. The agency is also researching radiation risks with whole-body computed tomography scanning, a medical imaging technique.

FDA activities are so wide ranging that the agency employs many different types of scientists, including chemists, biologists, microbiologists, pharmacologists, and statisticians. A chemist with the FDA, for example, may evaluate facilities, controls, and methods used to manufacture new drugs. He or she may write a summary of findings and review proposed labels to appear on the product. Other chemists may study dietary supplements and their effects on dieters.

To qualify for a job as an FDA scientist, you need a bachelor's degree or higher with a background in one or a combination of biological sciences, chemistry, pharmacy, physical sciences, food technology, nutrition, medical science, engineering, epidemiology, veterinary medical science, or related scientific fields. Computer programming skills are essential, as are communication and people skills, which scientists depend on to work with industry representatives, health care professionals, and educators. All FDA scientists need to keep up with rapidly advancing technologies and be prepared to deal with new public health risks (antibiotic-resistant bacteria and food-borne illnesses). Their goal is to advance public health by speeding innovations that can make medicines and foods more effective, safe, and affordable.

The FDA employs about 9,000 people around the country. The United States will continue to need scientists who want to help protect its citizens from harmful foods, drugs, and cosmetics.

find your future

foreign service officer

foreign service officer

The United States may currently be the world's leading superpower, but our country doesn't operate in isolation. At more than 250 locations around the world, America has set up embassies, small plots of American-owned land and buildings in foreign countries. Embassies not only act as the official residencies of U.S. ambassadors, but they are also important points of contact for Americans visiting on foreign soil and centers of American diplomacy. Employees who staff American embassies and assist the ambassador in each of these tasks are called foreign service officers (FSOs).

Historically, FSOs acted as generalists, taking on any duty they were assigned as they moved from post to post around the world. While some old-school FSOs still fill this role, most new hires from the past decade or so serve in one of five specialties: administrative, consular, economic, political, and public diplomacy. Workers generally stick to a set of duties particular to their specialty, but there is some overlap. For example, FSOs in any specialty may be expected to represent the United States at selected official functions, ceremonies, and meetings, or assist high-level American or foreign officers with visits to the embassy. Also,

Search It!
American Foreign Service Association at *www.afsa.org*

Read It!
State Magazine at *www.state.gov/m/dghr/statemag*

Learn It!
● Bachelor's degree or higher with liberal arts major or professional specialization such as law, medicine, or agricultural science
● Proficiency in foreign language preferred

Earn It
Average starting salary is $36,929. (Source: U.S. Department of State)

Find It!
The U.S. State Department employs many foreign service officers. Search for job leads at *www.state.gov*.

Get Started Now!

To start preparing for your career as a foreign service officer, do the following:
● Take courses in English, geography, and government to prepare for the foreign service exam.
● Work towards becoming fluent in at least one language other than English.
● Travel widely throughout the United States and overseas, if possible, to get exposure to many types of cultures.

Hire Yourself!

Imagine that you have been appointed as a public diplomacy officer to work in a country completely unfamiliar with the American education system. How would you explain your high school to a stranger who has never experienced anything like it? Selecting a few different topics, such as subjects, grades, and extracurricular activities, prepare a brochure that describes the "typical" American high school experience.

all FSOs must report to Washington from time to time and assist their ambassador in assessing and developing U.S. policies and programs.

Beyond these universal duties, FSOs in the administrative specialty operate the business aspects of their embassy. They might make sure that the embassy's bills are paid on time, manage the cleaning or secretarial staff, or set up contracts to lease, buy, or construct new facilities.

Those in the consular specialty concentrate on looking after the interests of American citizens who are traveling abroad. They handle the massive amounts of paperwork for issuing visas to foreign applicants. They also provide a variety of emergency and non-emergency services for U.S. citizens, such as replacing lost or stolen passports, arranging for emergency medical services, or mediating situations involving Americans who get arrested while overseas.

FSOs in the economic specialty work on issues revolving around money, such as the banking, trade and commerce, communication and transportation, economic development, and government finance of their host countries. They report significant developments in these areas to the State Department to help the United States develop economic policies.

Political specialty FSOs mostly follow political events within the host country, reporting significant events to the State Department. These workers are alert to the promotion of United States national interests in many areas and may intervene with foreign governments when circumstances warrant. They also convey official communications from the American government to host country officials when necessary.

Finally, FSOs in the public diplomacy specialty make sure that the lines of communication stay open between their host country and the U.S. government. They act much like public information officers, educating foreign officials about American policies and culture and collecting similar information about the host country.

No matter which specialty they work in, all FSOs are expected to act as official representatives of the United States. Having a strong knowledge of American society, culture, history, government, political systems, and the Constitution are mandatory for any of these positions. FSOs should also keep up with world geography, political, and social issues, and they should have a working knowledge of the language in their host country and major world history events. Even with all this know-how, not everyone is equipped to handle working as an FSO. Officers appointed to these positions work away from their homes in the United States for years at a time, usually taking their families with them to their posts located throughout the world.

Foreign service officers bring a broad array of academic and professional experience to their jobs. Many have bachelor's or advanced degrees in one of the liberal arts such as history, or political science. Others have highly specialized backgrounds in professional disciplines like law, medicine, or agricultural science or their training has been highly focused on a specific part of the world, such as Asian studies. Well-rounded individuals stand the best chance of getting hired. Strong general knowledge in many different areas can help applicants pass the foreign service exam, issued by the State Department and required for all FSO applicants. The exam tests an applicant's knowledge of a number of different areas, ranging from American arts and sports to basic economics and government. Those who pass a written section are called back to participate in the test's oral section, and a selected few who pass both sections are appointed to positions at foreign embassies. Those curious about which of the five foreign service specialties would be the best fit can complete an interactive on-line survey at the State Department website at *www.foreignservice.com/officer/careertrack*.

Search It!
U.S. Immigration and Customs
Enforcement at *www.ice.gov*

Read It!
Inside ICE newsletter at *www.ice.
gov/graphics/news/insideice/
index.htm*

Learn It!
● Entry-level positions in this field
require only a high school diploma or GED
● Higher education required to
advance

Earn It!
Median annual salary range is
$25,822 to $41,585.
(Source: U.S. Department of
Homeland Security Public
Information Office)

Find It!
All immigration officers work for
the federal government. Look for
job leads at USAJOBS, *www.
usajobs.opm.gov*.

find your immigration agent future

immigration agent

Of all the countries in the world where people most want to live, America ranks near the top of the list. Its cultural diversity and natural beauty also make it a top vacation destination for foreign visitors. Those who want to live and visit here, though, must abide by certain laws. For instance, immigration law requires that visitors from other countries stay only for a specified period of time before returning home. And those who are foreign citizens, but are working in the United States, must have their working papers in order.

Immigration agents work under the U.S. Department of Homeland Security to enforce these laws. Immigration professionals either work for Citizenship and Immigration Services (CIS) to help people legally immigrate or visit the United States, or they work for U.S. Immigration and Customs Enforcement (ICE) and handle investigations of violations of customs laws and immigration.

Immigration agents are like police officers who deal only with citizens of other countries. Many work at points of entry to our country—border crossings, seaports, and airports—trying to prevent illegal entry

Get Started Now!

To start preparing for your career as an immigration agent, do the following:
● Take courses in math, computer science, and foreign languages. These skills can help in tracking immigration statistics and communicating with foreign citizens.
● Start to bone up on basic immigration information available at the Immigration and Customs Enforcement website, *www.ice.gov*.

Hire Yourself!

Imagine that you are in charge of interviewing foreign Spanish-speaking citizens who are applying to become American citizens. Review the information provided in the U.S. Immigrations and Customs Enforcement's *Guide to Immigration* to come up with a list of 10 facts immigrants need to know about becoming a U.S. citizen. Feature these facts on a poster you create using poster board and markers or a computer graphic design program like Microsoft Publisher. For an extra challenge, use a free on-line language translation website such as *www.freetranslation.com* (or help from your school's Spanish teacher) to create a Spanish language version of the poster.

and checking paperwork. Other immigration agents work within the country apprehending illegal aliens. If they suspect that a foreign citizen is breaking immigration laws, officers have the authority to arrest that individual and bring him or her into custody.

Some immigration agents interrogate suspects or witnesses and conduct searches or raids on a suspect's home or workplace. Some patrol American borders to catch suspects who try to sneak across. Like regular police officers, immigration officers have authoritative positions that can often be stressful and dangerous. Some deal with human trafficking, contraband smuggling, and potential terror suspects. For self-protection, many of these officers carry a gun and, if necessary, are authorized to use physical force to subdue a suspect. If a case goes to trial, these officers are usually asked to testify in court about the details of the case. At the end of the trial, if a foreign citizen loses his or her case, immigration officers help deport that individual back to his or her original country.

Immigration agents also assist thousands of foreign citizens who wish to immigrate legally to America every year. These officers examine immigration applications and interview potential permanent immigrants. They also verify passports and issue visas for foreigners who are visiting America on a short-term basis. Some agents specialize in keeping records and preparing reports to keep track of how many foreigners visit America each year and from which countries they arrive.

Although having a bachelor's degree is not specifically required, candidates for these positions must be able to show, through a combination of education and experience, that they have the ability to handle difficult situations, make quick decisions, and take charge when necessary. Immigration agents depend on strong communication skills. A firm grasp

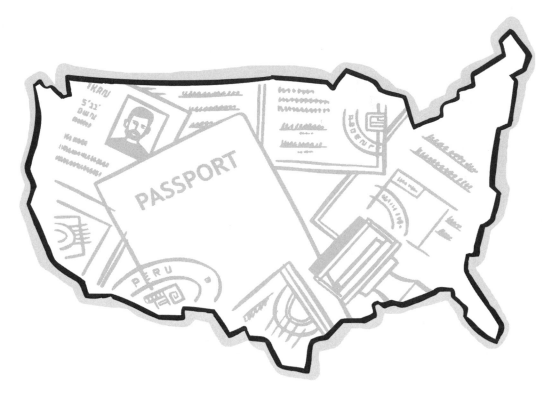

of the English language and some fluency in at least one foreign language can be extremely helpful in exchanges with citizens from abroad.

All immigration agents work for the federal government, which sticks to a strict list of civil service regulations in hiring. They must be U.S. citizens, younger than 37 years of age at the time of appointment, and possess a valid driver's license. They also must pass a three-part examination on reasoning and language skills. Once an immigration officer who fits these qualifications is hired, he or she trains for the position on the job and by attending sessions at an offsite academy.

Like all federal positions, job security for immigration agents is high. Plus, since September 11, 2001, our country has become more security-conscious, and that has led to an increasing demand for immigration services.

find your future

intelligence analyst

intelligence analyst

As they once said in the television program *The X Files*, "the truth is out there," and the job of intelligence analysts is to find it. These professionals look to discover the true intentions and actions of an enemy or potential enemy. They may monitor a potential threatening situation like the development of another country's nuclear program and provide regular updates to the federal authorities so they can take proper action. Intelligence experts provide the U.S. president and the National Security Council with information on which to base decisions concerning the conduct and development of foreign, defense, and economic policy, and the protection of U.S. national interests from foreign security threats. These professionals are on the frontlines of counterterrorism when it comes to our homeland security.

Intelligence experts work for all branches of the military, the Central Intelligence Agency (CIA), the Defense Intelligence Agency, the Department of Energy, the Department of Homeland Security, the Department of State, the National Security Agency, and other branches of government. Collectively they are known as the "intelligence community," and during a period of international crisis, analysts from different

Search It!
United States Intelligence Community at *www. intelligence.gov*

Read It!
Intel Briefing at *www. intelbriefing.com*

Learn It!
There are no set educational requirements, but undergraduate or graduate degrees in foreign culture studies, international relations, and mathematics are recommended. Foreign language skills can be especially helpful.

Earn It!
Median annual salary is $43,545. (Source: National Security Agency)

Find It!
Look for career possibilities at the Intelligence Careers website (*www.intelligencecareers.com*).

Get Started Now!
Uncover a career in the intelligence community:
- Courses in world history, politics, and foreign languages make for a good background in this field.
- Internships and work opportunities are available through the U.S. Intelligence Community. Check out Student Opportunity Programs at *www.intelligence.gov/ 0-student_opps.shtml*.

parts of the intelligence community may band together to form a task force to address a pressing security problem.

Intelligence analysts focus on foreign intelligence activities, international terrorist and international narcotics activities, illegal cyber-based activity, and other hostile activities directed against the United States. by foreign powers, organizations, persons, and their agents. They review incoming information, evaluate it, and write assessments detailing potential problems, predicting future trends, forecasting outcomes. Sometimes they identify intelligence gaps and decide how to gain more information. Analysts often rely on reports from field agents who collect intelligence information abroad, often putting themselves at great risk.

Intelligence specialists rely on electronic monitoring, copies of top-secret documents, human observation, and aerial photos taken by reconnaissance aircraft to assess foreign activity. Their goal is to determine the significance of the information: what are enemy capabilities, vulnerabilities, and probable causes of action? When information is captured, they store it on computers.

Although this work is primarily associated with protecting the United States, intelligence analysts can also work on a smaller level for local police departments. These analysts study criminal relationships and track suspects in criminal organizations. Using information gathered by detectives and officers, analysts can assess organized crime such as narcotics smuggling, money laundering, gangs, terrorism, and auto theft rings.

If you're analytically minded, concerned about U.S. security, and have an interest in immersing yourself in the language and culture of foreign countries, this could be the career for you. Sometimes the work will take these professionals to different locations to gather information, but analysts usually sit at a desk, using a computer to sift through data and write recommendations.

find your future

IRS (internal revenue service) agent

IRS (internal revenue service) agent

To keep our government up and running, the federal government collects trillions of dollars in taxes every year from individuals and corporations. The division of government responsible for collecting more than 90 percent of these taxes is the Internal Revenue Service (IRS), and IRS agents ensure that taxes are paid properly and promptly.

For many taxpayers—even those who have nothing to hide—the idea of being visited by an agent is unnerving. Agents typically examine financial documents and review the assets of individuals or companies. In the process, they may find that a party owes money and maybe even financial penalties for sending in taxes late or filing tax forms incorrectly. An audit, or a thorough review of taxes filed, may sometimes reveal

Get Started Now!

Use these strategies to get ready for a future as a tax agent:

- Math classes such as statistics and algebra will help.
- Get (or stay) tech-savvy. Those skills will definitely come in handy.
- If you've earned enough money in a part-time job, you may have to file your own taxes. (Check out the rules at *www.irs.gov*.) Try doing it yourself—it can give you personal insight into the tax process.
- If you really want to explore the career, look into interning or working part time at a professional tax preparer's office. One of the biggest tax service companies is H&R Block (*www.hrblock.com*).

Search It!
The Internal Revenue Service at *www.irs.gov*

Read It!
Tax, accounting, and audit news at *www.irs.gov/newsroom*

Learn It!
Bachelor's degree, preferably in accounting.

Earn It!
Median annual salary is $51,070. (Source: U.S. Department of Labor)

Find It!
Those interested in a position as an IRS agent should look for job vacancy announcements on *http:// jobsearch.usajobs.opm.gov*.

a case of tax fraud. Then IRS agents may have to pursue legal action against an individual or corporation. (The Mafia gangster Al Capone was locked up for not paying taxes, a crime known as tax evasion.)

IRS small business and self-employed division agents conduct examinations of persons and small businesses to determine what they owe in federal taxes. They make sure taxes paid out accurately reflect the revenues taken in. In the tax-exempt and government entities divisions, agents ensure that these organizations are complying with tax codes.

Technology is becoming increasingly important to the job of an IRS agent. Where in the past it may have been necessary to manually access and investigate data, now it is possible to access these same files electronically. Also, new software packages can summarize financial transactions and organize records much more efficiently than in the past.

A four-year degree with at least 30 hours of accounting classes is necessary to become an agent. As an entry-level employee, agents receive on-the-job training and instruction in topics such as tax law, report writing, fraud detection, taxpayer relations, and research and examination techniques. After the classroom instruction is complete, agents undergo a period of training under a more seasoned employee. This is followed by a period of computer training that focuses on the more sophisticated areas of tax law that relate to individuals, corporations, and partnerships.

Because this is a government position, salary is based on the grade at which a person is employed, and is determined by experience and geographic location. Most entry-level agents start out at grade GS-5, 7, or 9, and are eligible for promotion—provided job performance is up to par—once a year, up to grade GS-11. More detailed salary information can be found at *www.opm.gov/oca/payrates*.

You can also move laterally, which involves moving from a position in one department or division into one of equal responsibility in another department or division. For instance, an agent in the small business and self-employed unit might move over to criminal investigation (CI). CI is the unit that enforces tax, money laundering, and Bank Secrecy Act law. The division employs forensic accountants to locate evidence of tax fraud. In essence, they are IRS cops.

If you are planning a career in accounting or audit at the IRS, it helps to hone your math skills and cultivate an acute attention to detail—and a great deal of patience. After all, you will be poring over pages upon pages of financial documents with meticulous care, so it helps to have a high tolerance for detailed work. Report-writing skills and the ability to meet deadlines are also two very essential qualities. Agents must also be knowledgeable of the Financial Accounting and Standards Board (FASB) rules.

Job growth is expected to be about as fast as average through 2012 for accountants and agents. Still, as the saying goes, "the only two things certain in life are death and taxes," so there will always be a need for tax agents and collectors.

Read It!
Princeton Review online (*www.princetonreview.com/cte/profiles/dayInLife.asp?careerID=88*) offers an overview of this career

Learn It!
● Most lobbyists are college graduates with backgrounds in law, communications, or public relations
● Hands-on legislative experience

Earn It!
Average starting salary is $20,000. (Source: Princeton Review)

Find It!
Find postings from organizations that are currently hiring at *www.LobbySearch.com*. Look for a firm specializing in an area that matches your interests.

find your lobbyist future

lobbyist

President Ulysses S. Grant, after a long day in the Oval Office, used to escape the pressures of the presidency with a brandy and a cigar in the lobby of the Willard, a grand Washington, D.C., hotel located near the White House. It didn't take long for many legislators, leaders, and other would-be power brokers to catch on to this habit, and many would hang around in the lobby waiting for a chance to approach him about individual causes. Grant called these people "lobbyists," and the term is still used to this day to refer to people who work to influence legislation, or the passing of laws.

Anyone can be a lobbyist—the First Amendment to the Constitution guarantees that. When you write a letter, make a phone call, or pay a visit to Capitol Hill to meet with a member of Congress to discuss an issue you believe in, you are exercising your freedom of speech—and serving as a lobbyist.

Professional lobbyists are an essential part of the legislative process, and public officials would have a tough time making informed decisions without them. Colleges, churches, businesses, nonprofit organizations

Get Started Now!

If you want to work as a lobbyist, here's what you can do right now:

● Learn all you can about the legislative process. The publication *How Laws Are Made* is available on-line at *http://thomas.loc.gov/home/lawsmade.toc.html*
● Spend a summer working as a legislative intern. You'll find internship programs in your state listed on the website for the National Conference of State Legislatures at *www.ncsl.org*.
● Do some informal lobbying to get a taste for the process itself. The Lobbyist Network website (*www.lobbyist.net*) features resources that can help you get started.

and charities, local and foreign governments all rely on lobbyists to help communicate their interests to the government.

Lobbyists are paid by the people or organizations they represent and must register with the state and federal government. Corporate lobbyists work for individual companies while association lobbyists represent industry and trade associations. Some of the biggest employers of lobbyists are nonprofit organizations such as Greenpeace and the American Association of Retired Persons (AARP).

Indirect lobbying—sometimes called "grassroots organizing"—often involves working with the community to organize letter writing, e-mail, and phone campaigns, and forging alliances among various community groups. Grassroots lobbyists also communicate with the media to publicize the positions of the organizations they represent.

Direct lobbying means meeting face-to-face with government officials, such as members of Congress, to discuss upcoming legislation. However, working directly with public officials is only a small part of what lobbyists do. They spend the majority of their time involved with duties such as studying proposed legislation, working to build coalitions between groups, fund-raising, holding press conferences, and educating people about the implications of proposed laws and regulations.

Lobbyists put in long hours, often spending 40 to 80 hours a week on the job. Why are they willing to work so hard? Ultimately, the payoffs can be huge: successful lobbyists make powerful friends in high places and enjoy large salaries.

Lobbying is a profession that depends upon the art of persuasion. Lobbyists must be able to convince people of varying backgrounds of the worthiness of their cause. Charismatic individuals who are confident, outgoing, and able to communicate well in person and on paper make good lobbyists. If you're interested in this career, you'll want to gain some inside experience in government and lawmaking. Working in a legal or public relations firm can also be useful preparation for this job. Because so many different groups and organizations rely on lobbyists, a wide variety of positions are potentially available.

find your future
media relations specialist

Search It!

Public Relations Society of America (PRSA) at *www.prsa.org*

Read It!

Public Relations Strategist at *www.prsa.org/_Publications/ magazines/strategist.asp? ident=m2*

Learn It!

Many media relations jobs require at least a four-year degree in public relations, journalism, communications, or a related field.

Earn It!

Median annual salary is $41,710. (Source: U.S. Department of Labor)

Find It!

Media relations specialists can work for government, businesses, universities, and many other organizations. Look for job leads at USAJOBS (*www.usajobs.opm. gov*) and at the PRSA website (*http://www.prsa.org/ jobcenter/candidates/jobs.asp*)
.

media relations specialist

How would you like to speak for the president at a press briefing broadcast on national television? Could you handle turning a senator's ideas into an editorial mailed to thousands of newspapers? What about briefing the media about a groundbreaking NASA discovery? Whether taking someone else's place in the spotlight makes you nervous, excited, or both, it's a way of life for many government media relations specialists. These professional communicators do the talking and writing for government officials and agencies. When new policies are implemented by a government agency, the media specialist makes sure the changes are conveyed in a positive way to the public. If a politician is trying to get public support on a bill he or she authored, the media specialist tries to get coverage through television, radio, newspapers, and other forms of media.

As the "mouthpiece" for the government, media people must be strong speakers and writers. Because they are usually trying to get a message to the broadest audience possible, they are very well versed in

Get Started Now!

To spin your career as a media relations specialist, do the following:

- Take courses in English and government to learn how to communicate effectively about government issues.
- Join a drama or debate club to get comfortable speaking in front of large crowds.
- Read the newspaper to stay up-to-date on political and current events. You can get practice communicating your opinions by writing letters to your newspaper's editor.

Hire Yourself!

You have just been hired as your school's media relations specialist. One of your new position's most important duties will be writing press releases on the latest news and activities. Choose a current event that recently happened at your school and write up a press release. Make sure to interview key people involved in the event and include their quotes in your press release. Also include information on when the event happened, why it was important, and details that a reporter covering the event might want to know. You'll find a variety of useful resources on-line at the About.com website (*www.about.com*) and running searches using the words *public relations* and *press releases*.

how to get media attention. They issue press releases, organize press conferences, put together annual reports, and write speeches. They also stay in constant touch with journalists and other groups who can pass their messages on to bigger audiences.

People who work in media relations go by a variety of names that include press secretary, chief information officer, or public affairs specialist, to name a few. In government, these professional spokespeople form the link between administrative offices and the general public. They keep the community informed on the activities and accomplishments of government agencies and officials.

Although journalists are a media relations specialist's best connection to the public, they can also be the toughest audience. Since reporters can ask hard-hitting questions, people who work in media relations must be able to give detailed answers on the fly. Keeping calm under pressure and exuding confidence in a crisis are plusses in this job. The ability to communicate effectively under a variety of conditions— on the phone, in front of big crowds, or in print—is a definite must. Media relations specialists typically work a 40-hour week, but unpaid overtime is fairly common. Occasionally they'll be on call around the clock to handle breaking news or soothe a public relations disaster.

Although there is no standard route to becoming a media relations specialist, most government jobs in this field require applicants to have at least a four-year degree in communications, journalism, or a related major. Previous work experience is becoming increasingly important in snagging competitive positions; many employers now give special consideration to students with internships in some aspect of media relations.

find your future

meteorologist

meteorologist

Getting ready for a big softball game this week? How about a trip to the beach this weekend? No matter what you do outside, paying attention to the weather forecast will prevent you from getting caught in the rain. Weather information is important to many people, not just those headed on vacation. Knowing whether tomorrow will be rain or shine can affect industries that concentrate on shipping, air transportation, agriculture, and utilities. Lucky for people who work and play outside, today's technology can predict weather conditions up to 10 days in advance with a high degree of certainty. Meteorologists use this technology to forecast the weather, study the physical characteristics of different weather events, and analyze long-term climate trends.

Sometimes called atmospheric scientists, meteorologists study the atmosphere, the blanket of air that surrounds the earth. Those who make

Get Started Now!

To forecast your career as a meteorologist, do the following:
● Take classes in computer science, math, and physics to understand the tools meteorologists use to predict weather.
● Learn the basics of weather science by checking out Jetstream, the National Weather Service Online Weather School, *www.srh.noaa.gov/jetstream*.
● Become a weather junkie by reading daily weather forecasts in the newspaper, watching weather news reports on television, and just noticing changes in weather patterns in your own backyard.

Hire Yourself!

Track the weather in your community for a week in three ways. First, go on-line to a weather website such as **www.weather.com** and print out the week's forecast. Second, cut out the daily weather forecasts in your local newspaper. Third, take note of what the weather is actually like on a day-by-day basis. Make a chart comparing the predictions with the reality.

short- and long-range forecasts, called operational meteorologists, are the largest group of specialists in the field. These scientists collect data from satellites, radar, weather balloons, and weather stations throughout the world. They feed this information into computers to create complex models of conditions in the earth's atmosphere. Interpreting these models with a strong knowledge of climate theory helps meteorologists construct a forecast. Predicting the weather isn't an exact science, however. As tiny, unexpected changes arise in weather conditions, meteorologists tweak their models and interpretations to make forecasts more accurate.

Rather than predict the weather, some meteorologists specialize in researching past and current weather events. For example, physical meteorologists examine the atmosphere's physical and chemical properties. They study how air, water, and other molecules interact to form precipitation or types of pollution and investigate the mechanics of severe weather events, like hurricanes or tornadoes. Scientists called synoptic meteorologists develop new tools for weather prediction using computers and mathematical models of atmospheric activity. Climatologists look at past weather events, sometimes looking back over hundreds or millions of years, to determine climate trends. Environmental meteorologists study what role the weather plays in environmental problems like air pollution, flooding, or wildfires.

Since most weather centers stay open every day around the clock, many meteorologists are called upon to work during odd hours at night, on the weekends, or on holidays. A 40-hour week is average, but weather emergencies can call for plenty of overtime. Most meteorology work is done in a standard office environment, but some meteorologists spend part or all of their days collecting data from aircraft or in the field.

A bachelor's degree is the minimum requirement for any meteorology position. Atmospheric science is a relatively small field, so few colleges offer a full major in meteorology. However, most budding meteorologists combine classes in atmospheric science with physics, mathematics, or engineering classes. A degree in any of these areas is

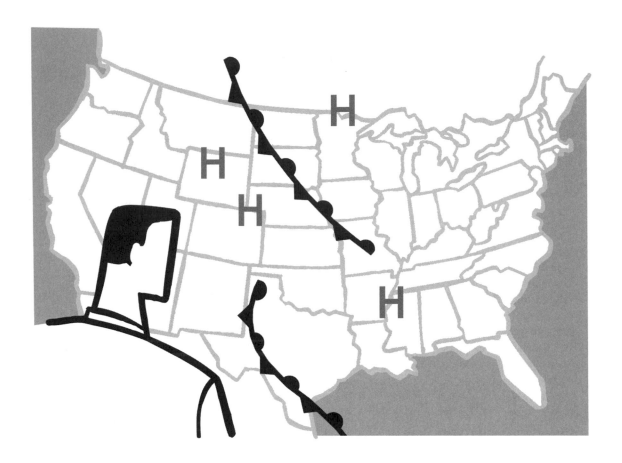

good preparation for graduate study in atmospheric science, an important step in getting a supervisory or research position.

The federal government is the largest employer of meteorologists, with most working in the National Oceanic and Atmospheric Administration's (NOAA) National Weather Service. In addition, several hundred meteorologists work as civilian forecasters for the armed forces through the Department of Defense. The remainder of meteorology jobs are in local government and the private sector, for businesses like private consulting firms and radio or television broadcasting stations.

find military serviceperson your future

Search It!
U.S. Department of Defense at
www.defenselink.mil

Read It!
Military Career Guide Online at
www.todaysmilitary.com

Learn It!
- Enlisted soldiers must have at least a high school diploma or GED
- Officers must have at least a bachelor's degree

Earn It!
Median annual salary starts at $12,300 for enlisted people and goes to $138,000 for a high ranking commissioned officer. (Source: U.S. Department of Defense)

Find It!
Find recruiters for all branches of the armed forces at **www. armedforcescareers.com**.

military serviceperson

Maybe you've seen those old-fashioned posters saying "Uncle Sam Wants YOU for the U.S. Army." But if you joined the Army, Navy, Air Force, Coast Guard, or Marine Corps, what would you do? The correct answer is, almost anything.

Together, all branches of the armed forces share the responsibility of protecting the United States and its allies from military threats posed by other countries or groups. Some military servicepersons fulfill that mission directly by driving tanks, firing artillery, flying planes, or performing

Get Started Now!

To gear up for your career as a military serviceperson, start now by doing the following:

- Take a wide variety of classes to prepare for the Armed Services Vocational Aptitude Battery, which tests a new recruit's job potential in many different areas.
- Join a sports team or start an exercise program to learn discipline and increase your physical fitness.
- Meet a recruiter to learn more about career opportunities in the military, but keep in mind that recruiters are likely to stress only the most positive aspects of military life. Do not make any official decisions until you've had a chance to consult with your parents, school counselor, or other trusted adults.
- Find out if your school sponsors a Junior ROTC (Reserve Officers' Training Corps) program. Participation in these programs often results in college scholarships and other very attractive benefits.

Hire Yourself!

The ASVAB, the army has recruited you to a position as an army recruiter! Your job is to get at least 30 people to enlist each month. What factors might attract someone to join the Army, and which ones might be definite drawbacks to enlisting? Write out a list of pros and cons that you might discuss with potential recruits. You can also search on-line for information on military occupational specialties (try *www.mosgame.com*) and then create a poster listing all the diverse opportunities.

other combat-related duties. But a large part of each military branch is devoted to keeping the military bases and posts up and running. Their occupations are as varied as installing plumbing in military buildings, acting as military police officers, maintaining ships or helicopters, or cooking meals in military mess halls. Although being in the military can be tough and dangerous work, especially for those in combat zones, the armed forces provides a decent salary, job training, and the opportunity to travel, all while providing an important service to your country.

Each branch of the military separates its employees into enlisted soldiers and officers. Enlisted personnel perform the majority of the military's day-to-day duties while officers supervise and manage the enlistees. Enlisting in any branch of the armed forces requires more than wanting to "be all you can be." Future servicepeople need to be between 17 and 35 years old. Those who are only 17 must have the consent of a parent or legal guardian. They also need to be U.S. citizens or aliens who have permanent resident status, have a birth certificate, and meet minimum physical standards, such as height, weight, vision, and overall health. No convicted felons are allowed. Almost all enlistees are high school graduates or have a GED, but the military does make a few exceptions for dropouts and provides free GED classes on almost every base. People interested in enlisting also need to pass a written exam called the Armed Services Vocational Aptitude Battery (ASVAB). The military uses scores from this test to sort new recruits into training programs.

Future soldiers who fit all these requirements enlist by meeting with a recruiter and signing a contract that lays out all the agreements between the military and the new recruit. Most active-duty programs have first-time enlistments of four years, although there are some two-, three-, and six-year programs. Right after enlistment, new recruits start six to 12 weeks of basic training where they get whipped into tip-top physical shape, learn strict lessons on military discipline, and get to know other recruits in their unit. After basic training ends, recruits get more specific training about their assigned specialties at military technical schools. Depending on their specialty, some soldiers skip this second level of training and learn their duties right on the job.

The story is much the same for soldiers who join the armed forces as officers, except that officers start with at least a bachelor's degree. Besides coming from regular colleges and universities, many officers come from United States military academies, like the U.S. Military Academy in West Point, New York, or the U.S. Air Force Academy in Colorado Springs, Colorado. After basic officer's training, they receive additional leadership training. Some enlisted personnel eventually become officers by earning college degrees while serving their regular duties. As a professional development motivation, the military provides tuition assistance for up to 75 percent of college costs.

There's no telling where a serviceperson will serve out his or her enlistment. With hundreds of military bases sprinkled around the world, enlisted personnel and officers could spend months or years in the United States, Germany, Korea, Japan, or anywhere else the United States has a military presence. Seeing the world can be a great incentive to join the military, but there are plenty of other benefits as well. In addition to basic pay, military personnel get free room and board, medical and dental care, a military clothing allowance, and 30 days' paid vacation a year. Many servicepersons also take advantage of a program called the New Montgomery GI Bill, which can provide tens of thousands of dollars to pay for college tuition once a soldier leaves the military.

A career in the military isn't for everyone. Many soldiers stay for only one enlistment period, and then take the skills they learned in the military to a new civilian job. But for those who enjoy life in the armed forces, a varied and challenging career is virtually guaranteed. With an all-volunteer military, recruits are always in high demand in each branch of the armed forces.

Search It!
The National Park Service at
www.nps.gov

Read It!
News at the Association of
National Park Rangers at ***www.
anpr.org/anprnews.htm***

Learn It!
- Bachelor's degree in natural
  resource management or related
  field
- Specialized training sometimes
  required

Earn It!
Median annual starting salary is
$20,908.
(Source: National Park Service)

Find It!
Those interested in a position as a
U.S. park ranger should visit the
Office of Personnel Management
at ***www.usajobs.opm.gov*** to
search for openings.

find your park ranger future

park ranger

Several times a month, the Kennesaw Mountain National Battlefield Park has an artillery demonstration with the park's cannons. Men dress in Civil War uniforms and educate an interested public in the workings of the cannons and the role that old-fashioned weapons played a century and a half ago in the war fought between the North and the South. Visitors uninterested in cannons can take a guided tour of the Mountain's trails, all the way to the top, or bring their binoculars for a three-hour bird walk. If it weren't for the work of park rangers, none of this would be possible.

The National Park Service employs 20,000 career and volunteer rangers, at over 370 sites in the United States, Guam, Puerto Rico, and the Virgin Islands. Like the parks in which they work, the tasks of a ranger are many and varied. They are responsible for forest fire control and prevention; researching and communicating a site's history; development of educational materials; enforcement of laws and regulations; and investigation of violations of these same regulations. For instance, a ranger may host a talk about the geological history of Old Faithful at Yellowstone National Park. Or perhaps she or he will prepare a slide show or hold a campfire talk. Or, as an example of an interpretive program, a ranger might demonstrate building a teepee for a group of elementary-school

Get Started Now!
Use these strategies to get ready for a future as a park ranger:
- Take as many classes in the earth sciences as you can.
- Volunteer at a local park. You could work as a "ranger in training" or a camp counselor for a summer!
- Knowing how to rough it in the wild is good skill for a would-be park ranger. Camping on your own or through a scouting troop can help you better understand how people and nature coexist in the forest.

Hire Yourself

You've just been hired as a park ranger. Your first task? To host a guided tour. Go on-line to the National Park Service website at *www.nps.gov/parks.html* and use the geographical search function to locate the national park closest to where you live. Use the information you find there and by researching other websites to prepare a 10-minute presentation about the park. Use PowerPoint or other types of visual aids to create an interesting and informative presentation.

children. They may also lead classes on such topics as hunting, boating, or water safety, among others. The job is not without its more routine, administrative duties as well. Sometimes, rangers are responsible for litter control or assigning sites to visitors at a campground.

There are a variety of other professions associated with the care and safety of our nation's parks. Park police, forest rangers, park security, game wardens and conservation officers all work to maintain the successful operation of the country's parks in various capacities. Park police and security may investigate violations such as leaving a campsite in disrepair, for instance. Conservation officers may track the number and condition of certain flora and fauna, and game wardens enforce hunting and fishing laws.

A love of the great outdoors is a common trait of park rangers, and most get to spend at least part of their work time outside. However, it is not uncommon for them to perform office work as well—especially as they advance to managerial positions, such as district ranger, park manager, or staff specialist. Once a ranger is hired, he or she is assigned to a park and is often reassigned to different sites around the country as they progress throughout their career.

An important part of any park ranger's job is educating the public about the value of protected sites and instilling a sense of respect for the wonders of Mother Nature. Many park rangers find this aspect of the job incredibly rewarding.

Some rangers get their start as a seasonal employee—this might mean taking on a summer job at a national park or campground, or volunteering their services. To be hired as a full-time permanent employee, candidates must have a bachelor's degree. Recommended areas of study include natural resource management, natural or earth sciences, horticulture, history, archaeology, park and recreation management, law enforcement, or museum sciences, just to name a few.

Search It!
The National Association of Police Organizations at *www.napo.org*

Read It!
Police magazine at
www.policemag.com

Learn It!
- High school graduate
- Two- or four-year degree in law enforcement is recommended and often required

Earn It!
Median annual salary for police officers is $43,390.
(Source: U.S. Department of Labor)

Find It!
Apply to local law enforcement agencies, or check websites such as *www.lawenforcementjobs. com*.

find your police officer future

police officer

On any given day a police officer may help track down a child separated from her mother in a crowded shopping mall; respond to the scene of a family dispute; make an arrest or issue a warning; stop drivers disobeying speed limits or stop signs; and respond to a report of a burglary, a noise complaint, or a crime in progress. Many police officers are assigned to patrol a specific area, maintaining order, helping people, and enforcing the law. They may patrol on foot, by car or motorcycle, or even on horseback.

Police officers have to be alert, perceptive, and able to notice and remember details. They need to prevent crimes, stop crimes in progress, and keep potentially volatile situations calm and orderly. When a crime has been committed, police officers pursue and arrest suspects, ultimately taking them to the local police precinct for processing. Arresting

Get Started Now!
- Like biking? Nearly half of all local police departments and 90 percent of those serving at least 100,000 residents use bike patrols for police and EMS personnel. Learn about the International Police Mountain Bike Association at *www.ipmba.org*.
- Like working with animals? Think about becoming a K9 officer. Learn more at the United States Police Canine Association at *www.uspcak9.com*, check out the qualifications needed to be a K9 trainer at *www.uspca3.com/trainers*, or see about becoming a foster family for a search and rescue dog from the National Disaster Search Dog Foundation at *www.searchdogsusa.org*.
- Look for civilian jobs or volunteer opportunities with your local police organization.
- Learn some common police codes at *www.police-central. com/police-codes.htm*.

officers are required to complete detailed reports that may be used by officers who follow up on the case, or by the attorneys who take part in the trial. Police reports usually include every aspect of the case, from details about the incident to the behavior of the suspect and the police at the time of the arrest.

Officers also help people in need. They might respond to an accident scene and provide emergency medical assistance until the ambulance arrives. Police officers also offer advice and services, such as giving a battered wife the name and location of a women's shelter. They also direct traffic in case of an emergency (like a flooded road) and talk to kids in schools about stranger safety.

An officer might work for a special unit, such as a K9 unit that uses dogs to sniff out criminals and perform rescue operations. Some officers work for the bomb squad, helping to find and safely dispose of explosives. Others are part of an elite team called Special Weapons and Tactics (SWAT). They provide extra protection, including snipers, during high-risk arrests and hostage situations.

Some police officers eventually become detectives. A detective collects facts, or evidence, for criminal cases. They examine crime scenes, collecting evidence like hair or clothing fibers and taking photographs of bloodstains, footprints, and anything that may seem relevant. They interview witnesses and protect the scene from being tampered with. A detective's tasks also include performing video surveillance, monitoring a criminal's Internet use, and examining police reports looking for clues. Using all of their research, detectives can give police their recommendation on how to proceed.

If you're thinking of joining forces with the police force, here's what you need to know. The minimum age to be a police officer is usually 20. You need a high school diploma or a GED, at the very least. Many police forces require either an associate degree or even a bachelor's in a field like criminal justice. After you apply, you've got to take a written test, a physical abilities test, and even a psychological exam. You also must be prepared to pass a drug test and background check. Personal

characteristics such as honesty, sound judgment, integrity, and a sense of responsibility are especially important so interviews by a senior officer or by a psychiatrist or psychologist might be involved in the interview process as well.

New recruits go through three to six months of training at a peace officer standards and training academy (POST). Training can be at either a local or regional facility, and can be a day program or a residential one. The POST program includes training in the laws that police officers need to enforce, directing and controlling crowds or motor vehicle traffic, self-defense, care and use of weapons, and special driving skills (important in high-speed pursuits).

Police officers are observers, enforcers, problem solvers, and negotiators. Good officers can calm people and get information from them. They are able to work with a wide range of people and community programs, and can inspire confidence in others.

find your future politician

politician

The United States is a republic with a representative government. We elect the people who will do the decision making for us. Our elections are democratic, which means that everyone votes directly for the candidates (except in presidential elections, where we vote for electors in the Electoral College, who then vote for president).

Politicians make laws and policies that affect every area of our lives, from the taxes we pay and the wars we fight, to what subjects we have to complete in order to graduate from high school. We elect members of our local schools boards, our legislators (at the local, state, and national level), some of our judges, and even some local administrative officials, such as the town clerk.

Getting elected is a big part of the job itself. In 2004, nearly 500,000 candidates ran for various elected positions. Many candidates use political consultants, such as pollsters, media strategists, and opposition researchers to help them in their election efforts. At the heart of a political campaign is the candidate's ability to convince people that he or she is the best person to represent their views and deserves their vote as well as their financial support. Successful candidates have very strong interpersonal skills.

Get Started Now!

- Learn the lingo! Get to know the language that politicians use. Check out the Glossary of Congressional and Legislative Terms at *www.thecapitol.net/glossary*
- A career as a politician means that you have to be very convincing in getting your constituents to vote for you. Take classes in public speaking, communications, and speechwriting.
- The Thomas website at *http://thomas.loc.gov* lists everything that is happening in Congress. Click on the link for "how laws are made," to learn the details of the process.

Search It!
Council of State Governments at *www.csg.org*, National Conference of State Legislatures at *www.ncsl.org*, and National Governors Association at *www.nga.org*

Read It!
Brush up on election basics with Ben's Guide to Government at *http://bensguide.gpo.gov/9-12/index.html*

Learn It!
Requirements of age, residency, and citizenship vary by office and location.

Earn It!
Median annual earnings vary from unpaid elected office to $400,000 for U.S. president.
(Source: The Capitol.net)

Find It!
Explore opportunities at State and Local Government on the Net at *www.statelocalgov.net*.

They are friendly, energetic, and able to communicate their ideas clearly and simply. They are extremely knowledgeable about a great many issues and able to analyze and compare different approaches to those issues.

Once in office, elected officials have many responsibilities. They prepare legislation, attend committee meetings, negotiate with other legislators to get legislation passed, and listen to testimony from interest groups that are affected by pending legislation. Legislators must know all the facts before they vote on anything. Sometimes they may have to travel to other parts of the world to see how American support there will be, or is being, used. Or, they may travel to see how another state or country is doing something to determine whether we want to do the same thing here.

The 535 members of the United States Congress work to get federal funding for their home districts, interact with the media to deliver their message to their constituents, and contribute to legislation, as a researcher and fact-finder, as a compromiser and support generator, or simply as a voter. There are many ways to become a politician. Some elected officials have backgrounds in law or senior management. Others have experience at a more local level. Still others become involved in the political process because they are passionate about an issue.

The best way to get a feel for legislation is to work with an advocacy group for something you feel strongly about. Many colleges and graduate schools also offer internships where students can work with a current legislator. And, of course, you can always volunteer to work on a candidate's election or fund-raising campaign.

find your future postal service worker

postal service worker

In 1639, a Boston tavern served as the first informal U.S. post office. The tavern received mail arriving from overseas, as well as mail en route from the fledgling states to England. Since that year, the United States Postal Service (USPS) has become ever-so-slightly more organized. Today, the USPS annually delivers hundreds of millions of letters, packages, and messages; serves at least 8 million businesses and 250 million Americans; and takes in hundreds of millions of dollars a year. At the core of this huge operation are the postal service workers.

To be sure, we have come a long way from post office taverns and the Pony Express. The post office employs more than 845,000 people, working in several different capacities. Postal workers may serve as postal service clerks, mail carriers, mail sorters and processors, or processing machine operators. They work in the country's most remote rural locations, as well as its most bustling cities.

Postal service clerks are the workers you see in the windows at your local post office. Among other things, they serve as cashiers selling stamps and money orders, and they collect letters and packages from customers. They are also responsible for answering questions about the different delivery methods and dealing with irate customers whose mail

Search It!
The United States Postal Service (USPS) at *www.usps.com*

Read It!
USPS news and events at *www.usps.com/common/category/news_events.htm*

Learn It!
● Basic competency in English
● Must pass written exam that tests ability to memorize information accurately

Earn It!
Median annual salary is $39,530. (Source: U.S. Department of Labor)

Find It!
Those interested in a position as a U.S. Postal Service worker can find out more at *www.usps.com/employment* or by visiting a local branch.

Get Started Now!

Use these strategies to get ready for a future as a postal service worker:

● Patience and interpersonal skills are essential. A job in retail will give you experience in customer service.
● Many jobs in the U.S. Postal Service are physically challenging, so it pays to stay fit.
● Volunteer to help sort mail in your school's office.

has either been lost or damaged. These postal workers have the most face time with the public, so it helps to have good people skills and a great deal of patience.

Mail sorters, processors, and processing machine operators process the mail. They load and unload mail trucks, process, sort "zip code + 4" (an automated process), and get mail ready to be delivered. Mail carriers then deliver the mail, after it has been readied by sorters and processors. Carriers are classified by their route (city, rural, suburban), and use a variety of delivery methods (trucks, satchels, carts). Carriers are also responsible for collecting money for postage-due and cash-on-delivery (COD) parcels. If they work a rural route, they may also sell stamps and money orders, as the nearest post-office may not be as accessible to country dwellers. By the same token, city carriers may have specialized responsibilities, such as delivering only parcels or only letters.

The job can be physically demanding and require patience and people skills. Postal cashiers must cope with frustrated customers, and sorters, clerks, and processors often have to lift heavy packages. Carriers often deliver under unfavorable weather conditions.

Workers are hired as one of three types of employee: casual (seasonal), part time, or full time. Depending on the capacity of the work, postal employees' schedules vary. Sorters and processors, for instance, usually work evenings and weekends. Carriers may start work as early as 4 A.M., but clerks maintain a relatively normal workday schedule.

To be eligible for a job as a postal worker, prospective employees need to be at least 18 years old and a U.S. citizen, or a resident-alien.

Hire Yourself

You've applied for a job as a postal worker in your community. Before the post office can offer you a job, you must pass the following two tests. First, go on-line to the Public Service Employee's Network website at *www. pse-net.com/PostOffice.htm*. Use a blank sheet of paper to record your results to the sample test questions.

Second, go on-line to the Activity Zone section of the National Post Office Museum's website at *www.postalmuseum. si.edu/activity/8c_decodebarcode.html*. Complete the on-line activity to decode the bar code. Once you've cracked the code, use it to create a bar code for your home zip code. Use a marker to neatly write your bar code on a blank sheet of paper. On a separate sheet of paper, explain the meaning of each of the symbols in the bar code.

They must pass a physical exam that includes lifting packages up to 70 pounds, as well as a drug test, and a written exam that measures speed and accuracy of memorization skills. Those who are put on a list are hired as openings arise over a two-year time period. Anyone who still wishes to be considered for positions after two years must go through a re-qualification process. Experienced postal workers can advance to positions such as that of manager or supervisor of different operations, or postmaster, who oversees all operations at a specific location.

Search It!
American Society for Public Administration at ***www. aspanet.org*** and National Forum of Black Public Administrators at ***www.nfbpa.org***

Read It!
Partnership for Public Service resources at ***www. ourpublicservice.org***

Learn It!
● Bachelor's degree in business, government, or public affairs and administration
● A master's in public administration or public policy

Earn It!
Median annual salary is $74,486. (Source: International City/County Management Association)

Find It!
State jobs are listed by the Council of State Governments at ***www. csg.org/CSG/States/jobs***. Jobs are also listed by the American Society for Public Administration at ***www.aspanet.org***.

find your future
public administrator

public administrator

Public administrators usually work for government agencies, but may also work for nonprofit institutions such as hospitals, community organizations, universities, and social service agencies. They almost always work in offices, and computers are essential to their jobs.

One large part of the job is keeping the agency or organization moving toward its goals. That can include organizing different departments, hiring and training personnel, setting policies and procedures, planning

Get Started Now!

Manage your way into a career in public administration with the following tips.

● Most government agencies rely heavily on computers to function efficiently. Become fluent in the use of common word processing and spreadsheet programs. Be able to do effective research on the Internet.

● As manager of a department or agency, you will need strong leadership skills. Get practice by organizing a project in your school, taking a leadership role in a school club, newspaper, or magazine, or volunteering with a community agency.

● Learn about the federal, state, and local government agencies that exist in your own areas of interest. You may be interested in a specific issue (such as energy, the environment, parks, or public education), or you may be interested in a set of skills (such as financial analysis, long-term planning, or research) that can be applied to many areas.

and controlling budgets, and organizing committees to take on different tasks. A public administrator may also develop policies, plan meetings and conferences, and coordinate activities of groups within the agency. Public agencies often use outside researchers and consultants who have specialized knowledge or experience that staff members may not have. Public administrators find or approve the hiring of such specialists, negotiate their contracts, and set guidelines for their work.

In many ways, public administrators are very similar to the executives who run companies or divisions of companies, and the same basic management skills are critical. Successful public administrators are good communicators, can organize and motivate others, can see the big picture, and can develop long-term plans and strategies. Public administrators must both understand financial management and budgeting, and they must be comfortable with reading and analyzing financial reports. On the other hand, there are some very important differences in the educations and responsibilities of these public administrators and corporate executives.

One difference between them is that a priority of corporate managers is to run their businesses to show a profit and increase the value of the shareholders' stock. Public agencies do not exist for the purpose of making a profit and do not have stock or shareholders. However, public administrators must be mindful of budgets and work hard to keep their organization's expenses in check in order to avoid having to cut important programs.

Public agencies have to focus on the political environment. Their administrators must succeed in having their priorities recognized by the government and in getting sufficient funds allocated to them. Public administrators have to thoroughly understand the current public policies, how those policies developed, and how the political systems work. They have to know about regulatory policies and how their agency fits into overall goals of the country.

CITY BUDGET

12,346.00	
22,599.45	330,789.33
34,567.67	466,456.00
5,667.88	56,789.90
4,555.66	45,890.55
34,621.00	35,900.55
	6,899.25

While a few schools do offer undergraduate majors in public affairs and administration, most people in this field get their specialized training in graduate school. The National Association of Schools of Public Affairs and Administration (NASPAA) offers information on various graduate programs at *www.naspaa.org*.

Students interested in this management side of public service are usually advised to complete a master's of public administration (MPA) degree. Those interested in developing and implementing policies, whether as consultants or full-time employees of a government or agency, usually complete a master's of public policy (MPP) degree. In MPP programs, students focus on working with quantitative and qualitative information and data.

Careers in public administration offer an opportunity to contribute to your country (or state, county, or city) without having to run for re-election every few years. They offer a wide range of challenging careers, good salaries, and excellent benefits. To learn more about specific jobs, go to the Partnership for Public Service at *www.ourpublicservice.org* and click on the Agency Profiles and Profiles in Public Service icon.

find your future public attorney

public attorney

In the words of the popular television show *Law and Order*: "In the criminal justice system, the people are represented by two separate yet equally important groups—the police who investigate crime, and the district attorneys who prosecute the offenders." District attorneys or prosecutors are public attorneys who represent the government's perspective in a court case. Public defenders represent the interests of those accused of criminal activity who cannot afford to pay for their own legal counsel. Both types of attorneys are employed by local, state, or federal governments.

In simple terms, a prosecutor's job is to prove that an accused person is guilty of breaking the law, while a public defender tries to prove that the accused in not guilty. These types of lawyers work for all levels of government—from counties to states on up to the federal government—and handle cases involving a wide range of criminal activity that includes domestic violence, robbery, illegal drug sales, murder, and organized crime. An important tenet of our nation's criminal justice system hinges on the principle that a person is innocent until proven guilty. Thus, it is imperative that both types of lawyers do their jobs well lest an innocent person be wrongfully convicted or a guilty person go unpunished.

Get Started Now!
Use these strategies to get ready for a future as a public attorney:
- Take courses in history and English to help develop the research and reasoning skills demanded of a lawyer.
- Join your school's debate team to learn how to present logical arguments from both sides of an issue.
- Contact your local D.A.'s office to inquire about internships.

Search It!
The American Bar Association at **www.abanet.org**

Read It!
Legal news on-line at the *National Law Journal* at **www.nlj.com**

Learn It!
- Four-year college degree and completion of law school
- Successfully secure bar admission through a state board of bar examiners

Earn It!
Starting annual earnings range from $25,000 to $55,000. (Source: **www.legalauthority.com**)

Find It!
Explore employment options in public law at **www.legalauthority.com**. For information on opportunities with the federal government visit the Office of Personnel Management website at **www.usajobs.opm.com**.

The public defender is an elected or appointed attorney who is regularly assigned by the courts to defend people who cannot afford a lawyer. While there are federal public defenders and some states have their own public defenders, most work for county governments. These lawyers are obligated to accept all cases appointed to them, so they are often under the strain of a heavy workload, and have more than one case to work on at any one time. Like prosecutors, public defenders begin trying misdemeanor cases, and move on to more serious cases as they acquire understanding and experience.

Each county also has an elected district attorney (D.A.) or prosecutor who determines when to file charges against individuals accused of crimes and prosecutes those cases in court. In larger counties, the district attorney is in charge of a staff of other lawyers called assistant district attorneys. A prosecutor's office generally has specialized divisions which focus on specific types of crimes such as domestic violence, fraud and corruption, homicide, and narcotics. In smaller district offices, attorneys may get to try their hand at a broader range of cases.

Federal prosecutors work in Washington, D.C., at the Department of Justice and at U.S. attorney's offices nationwide. These attorneys prosecute those accused of violating federal laws and may try cases involving narcotics, organized crime, tax evasion, or insider trading.

Both prosecutors and public defenders must be able to apply the law to each specific case. They spend a great deal of time doing legal research, drafting legal documents, investigating facts associated with legal matters, and interviewing witnesses. All of this happens outside the courtroom. This intense behind-the-scenes work occurs before they enter a court room to present evidence or defend a client.

In addition to prosecutors and public defenders, all levels of government employ huge numbers of attorneys to keep them out of legal trouble. These attorneys serve as legal counsel for virtually every government agency at city, county, state, and federal levels. While their actual jobs are as varied as the agencies they serve, this type of work typically involves drafting new laws, enforcing existing laws, and ensuring that the agency is in compliance with the law.

Hire Yourself

You be the judge. Go on-line to the Court TV website at *www.courttv.com/trials/famous* and choose one of the featured famous court cases. Review the evidence and write a one-page summary expressing your opinion on the outcome of the case.

All types of lawyers must go to school for seven years—the first four as undergraduates majoring in pre-law, history, political science, or other related subject and the final three years in law school. After completing law school, they must pass a six-hour written exam administered by the American Bar Association (ABA).

Getting into law school involves an incredibly competitive process. Only those with the highest grades and most impressive resumes gain admission. All ABA-approved law schools require applicants to take the Law School Admission Test (LSAT), and usually offer J.D. (juris doctor) programs that last three years. The first half of law school is devoted to core classes, such as constitutional law, property law, and torts, for example. The second half of law school is devoted to specialized classes, like environmental or intellectual property law.

Search It!
The Centers for Disease Control and Prevention (CDC) at *www.cdc.gov*

Read It!
Preventing Chronic Disease on-line journal at *www.cdc.gov/pcd*

Learn It!
● Master's degree in public health or related field
● Completion of CDC's three-year Public Health Prevention Service training program

Earn It!
Median annual starting salary is $35,519.
(Source: Centers for Disease Control and Prevention)

Find It!
Those interested in a position as a public health official or prevention specialist can find employment information at *www.cdc.gov/epo/dapht/phps/applicant.htm*.

find your public health official future

public health official

In many parts of the world AIDS continues to be a major health threat. In the United States alone, 100,000 new cases of cancer are diagnosed each year. These are just two of countless health risks that threaten the well-being of the world's citizens. To fight against these diseases and promote better health, governments of all sizes rely on public health officials. Public health officials work at all levels of government—for counties and states in departments of health, for the federal government in places like the Centers for Disease Control and Prevention (CDC), and for the world at large with agencies like the United Nation's World Health Organization.

Overall, the job of public health officials is to keep the world's people safe and healthy. To accomplish this mission public health efforts center around three main types of activity: disease prevention and control, environmental health, and health promotion and education activities.

The following scenario illustrates how these activities might come into play in response to a specific health-related situation. A team of public health officials were asked to find ways to decrease the incidence levels of asthma among third and fourth graders in a community in New

Get Started Now!
Use these strategies to get ready for a future as a public health official:
● Math and science classes are key to preparing you for many types of health care careers.
● Find out more about world health issues at the World Health Organization website at *www.who.int/en*.
● Volunteer at a local hospital or public health clinic to learn more about the types of health issues prevalent in your community.

Hire Yourself

Your first task as a public health official at the CDC is to speak to a group of school administrators about the importance of measles, mumps, and rubella (MMR) vaccination. Prepare a fact sheet on how all three are contracted; their symptoms; and worst-case scenarios. Be sure to include at what age children should be vaccinated. Prepare your comments as you would an oral presentation. Here is a website that will help get you started: *www.cdc.gov/nip/ vaccine/MMR/default.htm*. Also, you'll find many websites that discuss MMR by using a favorite search engine such as *www.google.com* to conduct an Internet search.

Mexico. First they investigated the levels of asthma "triggers" in student's homes to identify ways to prevent asthma attacks. They also administered surveys to students and parents (kindergarten through 12th grade) to determine available health resources and studied data about the rate incidents of asthma in the area. After analyzing all the research, these public health officials assisted in the development of education efforts through school officials, health care providers, and local medical authorities to make sure information on how to treat and prevent asthma reached students and parents. As part of the education effort, a bilingual website was set up where members of the community could go for free medical advice.

Since public health requires such a broad and diverse array of skills, public health officials tend to be specialized in both their training and their work assignments. Applied and laboratory is one such area of specialization. This area involves using the latest techniques and technologies in a quest to discover solutions to the world's most perplexing health problems.

Epidemiology is another area of specialization. Epidemiologists work throughout the world to study why and how specific diseases spread in specific situations and locations. Those specializing in health communication use a variety of media, interactive technologies, and audience research techniques to deliver credible health and safety information to specific populations of people. Other public health officials concentrate on health policy research and development. Childhood immunization requirements are an example of the results of this type of work.

Public health informatics is an emerging area of specialization that focuses on applying the latest computer and information technology to real health problems.

In addition, other public health officials specialize in prevention as it relates to a particular category such as immunization, behavior change, lifestyle modification, HIV/AIDS, and injury and disability prevention. Still others work in leadership capacities managing programs and professionals and cutting through the bureaucratic red tape often associated with securing funding necessary to keep the world healthy and safe.

Those who enter public health typically have a desire to help others and are interested in the study of biology, science, and health care. To start off on this career path, candidates must first have a master's degree in public health or a related field (health education, for example), excellent academic records in the career-specific courses, such as biostatistics or microbiology (study of bacteria, fungi, viruses, etc.), and two to three years' experience in the field of epidemiology or public health management.

Currently there is a shortage of public health officials, which means that there is likely to be strong demand for public health officials in the future. The public health arena provides exciting opportunities for health care professionals who want to truly make a difference—whether close to home or in some far-flung corner of the world.

find your future: public policy advisor

public policy advisor

Poverty, the environment, health care, education, AIDS—you've probably heard political leaders discuss all these issues. The government establishes public policies for dealing with issues like these that affect society as a whole. Public policy advisors help develop plans of action on a wide range of social and political issues. They work in all levels of government and in nonprofit organizations that promote policy change. Advisors may work to maintain clean air and water standards. They may draft proposals to ensure that Social Security provides funding for generations to come. They may collaborate with officials to improve our health care system.

Although policy advisors become very specialized, focusing on a specific issue, their jobs often share similar features. All policy advisors analyze and evaluate complex information to solve major problems. They rely on quantitative and qualitative data to develop, assess, and evaluate what needs to be done. For instance, if they were deciding on education plans for inner city children, they might review case histories

Get Started Now!

Follow these policies to start a career in this field:

- Any courses in American history, politics, economics, and sociology can provide a solid foundation for a potential policy advisor.
- Hone effective communication skills by taking courses in speech, debate, and creative writing.
- Working side-by-side with policy makers is the best way to see if the field is for you. Check into internships with organizations that address an issue that interests you. Also, look for opportunities and information with the American Institutes for Research at *www.air-dc.org* and Political Research Associates at *www.publiceye.org*.

Search It!
National Association of Schools of Public Affairs and Administration at *www.naspaa.org*

Read It!
The Public Policy Analysis and Management newsletter at *www.appam.org/news/newsletter*

Learn It!
A master's degree in public policy from any of the 250 U.S. university programs in public affairs, public policy, public administration, and public management.

Earn It!
Median annual salary is $65,000. (Source: The H. John Heinz III School of Public Policy and Management)

Find It!
Check for government job opportunities at *www.USAJOBS.opm.gov* or at *www.careersingovernment.com*.

Hire Yourself!

The local school board would like to appoint a student policy advisor. To be considered for the job, applicants must identify three major issues facing your high school and recommend what the official school policy should be. To develop a knowledgeable policy, you will have to research what current policies are already in place. For example, you might ask an administrator what type of recycling program the school uses and then make recommendations for change based on the current operation.

of how effective school choice has been. If advisors were recommending a change in Social Security, they might project the financial effects of changing the retirement age from 65 to 70 years.

To do the needed research and draw up proposals, advisors benefit from a background in statistics, data analysis, public finance, budgeting, microeconomics, and macroeconomics. Colleges that teach public policy have developed very specific training on how to conduct research and evaluate programs.

Often policy advisors get involved with grant writing, fund-raising, and processing legal forms. These professionals may mostly focus on the "big picture," but sometimes they get closely involved with the individuals most affected by the policy. An advisor at a city department of human services, for instance, may directly respond to problems of the poor, disabled, homeless, elderly, and minorities.

At the core of this profession is a desire to make a difference in the world and improve society as a whole. Someone with a deep conviction about a particular social issue—whether it be the environment or space exploration or some other social cause—may find great satisfaction in this type of work.

Some policy advisors start out working in community groups and nonprofit organizations, such as the Consortium for Latino Health or Greenpeace. Although people enter this field from varied backgrounds, many start out with an interest in government, economics, sociology, or philosophy. Some go on to earn law degrees because an understanding of legal issues can aid in developing and changing policy.

According to the U.S. Bureau of Labor Statistics, nearly 40 percent of all public policy graduates are employed in government positions, and opportunities are expected to grow over the next few years. As the world's population continues to swell, social issues become more complex and the need for policy advisors will be greater than ever.

find **your** **social worker** **future**

social worker

Sometimes life presents problems that are too much for people to handle on their own. When life gets tough, people often turn to social workers for help. These government workers are specially trained to help clients deal with personal crises, such as inadequate housing, unemployment, serious illness, disability, or substance abuse. They may also counsel families experiencing serious domestic conflicts that may include physical or sexual abuse.

There are three main types of social work. One type involves case work, where social workers interact on a case-by-case basis with individuals or families. In most situations social workers are responsible for multiple cases at any given time. Another type of social worker focuses on group work, which involves a variety of rehabilitation and recreation services. They work in places where groups of people are typically found such as housing projects, hospitals, and schools. The third type is called community organization work and it involves working with a specific neighborhood or community to address specific concerns.

According to the National Association of Social Workers, professional social workers are found in every facet of community life—in

Get Started Now!

To nurture your career as a social worker, do the following:

- Take classes in psychology, speech, and a foreign language—all will help to better understand patients' problems and communicate with them effectively.
- Look into volunteer and internship options at your community's office on aging or children and family services.
- Volunteer or find out about student aide positions in your school guidance office to get some hands-on experience in a helping capacity.

Search It!
National Association of Social Workers at *www.naswdc.org*

Read It!
Social Work Today magazine at *www.socialworktoday.com*

Learn It!
- A master's degree in social work or a related field
- For a listing of accredited social work programs, visit the Council on Social Work Education at *www.cswe.org*

Earn It!
Median annual salary is $33,150. (Source: U.S. Department of Labor)

Find It!
Look for job leads at the Social Work Job Bank, *www. socialworkjobbank.com*.

schools, hospitals, mental health clinics, senior centers, elected office, private practices, prisons, the military, corporations, and in numerous public and private agencies that serve individuals and families in need. They often specialize in one or more of the following practice areas: mental health therapy, disaster relief, adoption and foster care, child welfare services, eating disorders, genetics, family planning, gerontology services, and domestic violence.

The majority of social workers specialize in dealing with children, family, or schools. Many of them are employed by child welfare, family services, or gerontology offices of local governments. These social workers may help single parents arrange adoptions or find foster homes for neglected, abandoned, or abused children. In schools, social workers might run support groups for students with learning disabilities or help develop programs to deal with teenage pregnancy, misbehavior, or truancy. Social workers who specialize in the medical or public health field are typically employed by hospitals or nursing facilities, where they provide support for patients dealing with acute, chronic, or terminal illness. A third group of social workers specializes in treating patients with mental health or substance abuse problems, helping them get into rehabilitation programs or finding work and housing. They may work in treatment facilities or in local government offices.

Regardless of their specialty, all social workers perform many of the same general tasks. They conduct intake interviews, which involves meeting with a new client to determine the types of needed services. Based on this information, they may consult with other social workers or specialists, like doctors or lawyers, to work out possible solutions to a client's dilemma. Once all the information has been gathered and all viable options considered, the social workers put together an action plan to guide their ongoing work on specific cases.

A bachelor's degree is the minimum requirement for many social work positions. Many colleges and universities offer majors in social

Hire Yourself!

In addition to helping individual clients with their problems, many social workers are also activists for particular social problems in their communities. Identify an issue facing students at your school such as cheating, bullying, or eating disorders. Research your issue on the Internet or at the library. Create a fact sheet that identifies the problem, suggests possible solutions, and provides a list of helpful local resources.

work, but related study in areas such as psychology or sociology may be acceptable for some jobs, especially in small community agencies. Although a bachelor's degree can get you into the field, a master's degree has become the standard for many specialty positions, and most research or management jobs require a doctorate. In addition to a degree, all states and the District of Columbia require social workers to meet additional licensing, certification, or registration requirements. These vary by state.

According to the U.S. Department of Labor's Bureau of Labor Statistics, social work is one of the fastest growing careers in the United States. The profession is expected to grow by 30 percent by 2010 and nearly 600,000 people currently hold social work degrees. Those who specialize in gerontology are finding many opportunities because of the aging baby boomer population, while work is also plentiful for those who specialize in substance abuse. Social worker is often the career of choice for people who want to help others overcome some of life's most difficult challenges.

find transportation your manager future

Search It!
U.S. Department of Transportation at *http://careers.dot.gov* and the Federal Transit Administration at *www.fta.dot.gov*

Read It!
The *Journal of Public Transportation* at *www.cutr.usf.edu/index2.htm*

Learn It!
● A bachelor's degree in traffic engineering, transportation planning, civil engineering, public administration, or related field
● Supervisory experience in public works

Earn It!
Median annual salary is $66,950. (Source: International City/County Management Association)

Find It!
Search job postings at the International City/County Management Association website at *www.icma.org*.

transportation manager

Whether you're in New York, Chicago, Miami, or any city in the country, a public transportation system helps you get you where you need to be via a sophisticated system of buses, trains, roadways, and bike paths. Transportation managers and directors make sure a city's traffic flows smoothly and safely.

On a national level, the U.S. Department of Transportation (DOT) tries to ensure a fast, safe, efficient, accessible, and convenient transportation system that meets our national interests and quality of life. It has several divisions to handle the nation's highways, rail, waterways, and air travels.

Most public transportation managers, however, work within local governments as part of an overall city or town management team. As department heads, they have major supervisory and administrative roles. A leadership position such as this requires broad experience and knowledge of the issues at hand. Managers must plan, organize, direct, and promote activities regarding transportation. They know all about current

Get Started Now!
Get on the road to a career in transportation.
● Volunteer to help direct traffic at school events or at your favorite place of worship.
● Many websites deal with public transportation. Be sure to visit the International City/County Management Association at *www.icma.org* and Intelligent Transportation Systems (ITS) News at *www.nawgits.com/icdn*.
● Get a part-time job or internship working within your local department of transportation.

modes of transportation, including street and traffic operations, bicycle systems, pedestrian requirements, and mass transit operations. To ensure safety, a transportation manager might look into where more lighting is needed to help drivers at night, or if traffic signs are posted in areas where there has been a rise in accidents. They must be very familiar with all traffic laws and regulations.

Mathematical and accounting skills are vital to this profession. Traffic managers analyze reams of data and surveys regarding public transportation use and needs. When and where do the heaviest traffic patterns occur? What are the most cost-effective and environmentally friendly ways for citizens to travel for work, for shopping, and for leisure activities? The manager conducts cost analysis and statistical computation that can provide these answers. Making improvements generally costs money, so a transportation manager must know how to work within a budget and allocate funds accordingly. Knowing materials, methods, and techniques for construction helps in making budgetary decisions.

To develop transportation plans, managers communicate with other city employees, city management, contractors, public officials, and the general public. In general, they are concerned with meeting the needs of the people, so they want to keep in touch with public opinion. If parking is difficult downtown, managers may propose new public parking lots. If bicyclists complain of inadequate parking, managers may install more public bike racks. Whether repairing a bridge or installing a new light rail system, managers must ensure that all projects comply with safety standards, operating procedures, federal and state regulations, and city policies. They are skilled at interpreting blueprints, schematic drawings, layouts, and other visual aids.

To get the work done, managers oversee a team and must be effective at delegating responsibility and assuring that their employees get the jobs done. Those who have leadership experience definitely excel in this position. A background in urban planning and public administration helps in determining how cities can be more efficient and how to work within a bureaucracy. Those who are highly organized, good decision-makers who want to make life better for their fellow city residents might consider this career. Opportunities can change depending on the health of local government budgets, but many cities are looking to invest in transportation systems that can make their locales more productive and accommodating to the people who live and work there.

find your urban planner future

urban planner

Left to their own devices, cities and suburbs can get very chaotic and difficult to live in. Urban sprawl results in too much traffic, not enough parks, and buildings that almost seem to be constructed on top of each other. The job of the urban planner is to ease the pressures of living in cities and towns, improving life by carefully deciding where each building, park, street, and even sewer grate will be placed.

To create long- and short-term plans for community growth and renewal, planners analyze how land is currently developed to help local governments solve social, economic, and environmental problems. They examine data on specific issues such as public transportation and housing costs. Then using detailed maps and computer programs, these professionals detail how to make living in the community more healthful, efficient, convenient, and attractive. Many specialize in a particular area, such as transportation, historic preservation, or environmental

Search It!
American Planning Association at
www.planning.org

Read It!
URBAN magazine at *www.arch.*
columbia.edu/up/magazine

Learn It!
- At least a master's degree in urban or regional planning or a related field
- Check out accredited programs on-line at the Association of Collegiate Schools of Planning (*www.acsp.org*)

Earn It!
Median annual salary is $49,880.
(Source: U.S. Department of Labor)

Find It!
Most urban planners work for local government agencies. Look for job leads at Planetizen, *www.*
planetizen.com.

Get Started Now!

To start planning your career as an urban planner, do the following:

- Take courses in math, computer science, and geography to help you understand spatial relations and land use.
- Join a drama or speech club to learn how to communicate your ideas clearly and effectively to an audience.
- Collect city maps and pay close attention to how a city is laid out. Where are the parks, major roadways, firehouses, police stations, water treatment plants, and libraries?
- Many websites discuss issues of urban planning. A great place to start is Cyburbia, the urban planning portal at *www.cyburbia.org*.

issues. A planner may focus on preserving a block of landmark buildings or revitalizing a neighborhood that has slumped into urban decay.

Day-to-day work can vary, but most urban planners start a new project by visiting the site under development. They examine resources that already exist in the area, such as schools, libraries, or bus lines, to determine to what degree these facilities meet existing needs. When a population grows, that can change the demand for services, so planners brainstorm where new resources may be necessary and they use computer models to visualize how their ideas might work.

Whether they're helping to build a new park or a road system to ease traffic, urban planners consult with many other experts—government authorities, civic leaders, social scientists, land developers, and the general public. Urban planners rely on diplomacy and well-honed communication skills to persuade government officials, the public, special interest groups, and corporations that their plans are best for all parties concerned. Because laws and building regulations may affect the developments, urban planners also consult with lawyers. Planners must stay up to date with changing zoning codes, building codes, and environmental regulations. When the time comes to set their plan in action, planners collaborate with builders to make sure they follow the appropriate laws as well as to make sure the plan stays on track.

Urban planners need to be able to think in terms of spatial relationships and picture the effects of their designs before land development starts, so analytic ability and creativity are important. They often work under pressure—meeting tight deadlines and dealing with special interest groups who are affected by proposals. Because they frequently travel to inspect new project sites or to sit in on community meetings, planners sometimes work irregular hours and in many different environments.

Hire Yourself!

Imagine that you have been hired to evaluate land use at a local playground. Visit the site during a period of heavy use, for example, recess on a weekday. Are there enough resources to satisfy most of the playground's users? Which pieces of equipment are used most often, and which are left untouched? Interview a few of the children and teachers about how they wish the playground could be changed. Write a report on what changes you'd make to the playground and why, then sketch out a design for a new playground based on your findings and present it to your class.

Although most urban planners are employed by city, county, state, and federal agencies, some work for architects, engineers, and real estate developers. These employers usually prefer workers who have advanced training, and most entry-level jobs require a master's degree. Many start with a bachelor's in planning, then get a master's in urban or regional planning, or in a related field, like urban design or geography. These programs often incorporate classroom time with workshops and lab time where students learn to solve real-world planning problems. Many local government offices offer internships, which often lead to full-time employment. Job prospects for qualified urban planners are currently high as the nation's communities continue to grow and evolve.

Big Question #5:
do you have the right skills?

Career exploration is, in one sense, career matchmaking. The goal is to match your basic traits, interests and strengths, work values, and work personality with viable career options.

But the "stuff" you bring to a job is only half of the story.

Choosing an ideal job and landing your dream job is a two-way street. Potential employers look for candidates with specific types of skills and backgrounds. This is especially true in our technology-infused, global economy.

In order to find the perfect fit, you need to be fully aware of not only what you've got, but also what prospective employers need.

The following activity is designed to help you accomplish just that. This time we'll use the "wannabe" approach —working with careers you think you want to consider. This same matchmaking process will come in handy when it comes time for the real thing too.

Unfortunately, this isn't one of those "please turn to the end of the chapter and you'll find all the answers" types of activities. This one requires the best critical thinking, problem-solving, and decision-making skills you can muster.

Big Activity #5:
do you have the right skills?

Here's how it works:

Step 1: First, make a chart like the one on page 128.

Step 2: Next, pick a career profile that interests you and use the following resources to compile a list of the traits and skills needed to be successful. Include:

- Information featured in the career profile in this book;
- Information you discover when you look through websites of any of the professional associations or other resources listed with each career profile;
- Information from the career profiles and skills lists found on-line at America's Career InfoNet at **www.acinet.org**.

Briefly list the traits or skills you find on separate lines in the first column of your chart.

Step 3: Evaluate yourself as honestly as possible. If, after careful consideration, you conclude that you already possess one of the traits or skills included on your list, place an *X* in the column marked "Got It!" If you conclude that the skill or trait is one you've yet to acquire, follow these directions to complete the column marked "Get It!":

- If you believe that gaining proficiency in a skill is just a matter of time and experience and you're willing to do whatever it takes to acquire that skill, place a *Y* (for yes) in the corresponding space.
- Or, if you are quite certain that a particular skill is one that you don't possess now, and either can't or won't do what it takes to acquire it, mark the corresponding space with an *N* (for no). For example, you want to be a brain surgeon. It's important, prestigious work and the pay is good. But, truth be told, you'd rather have brain surgery yourself than sit through eight more years of really intense science and math. This rather significant factor may or may not affect your ultimate career choice. But it's better to think it through now rather than six years into med school.

Step 4: Place your completed chart in your Big Question AnswerBook.

When you work through this process carefully, you should get some eye-opening insights into the kinds of careers that are right for you. Half reality check and half wake-up call, this activity lets you see how you measure up against important workforce competencies.

Big Activity #5: **do you have the right skills?**

skill or trait required	got it!	get it!

more career ideas in government and public service

Careers featured in the previous section represent mainstream, highly viable occupations where someone with the right set of skills and training stands more than half a chance of finding gainful employment. However, these ideas are just the beginning. There are lots of ways to make a living in any industry—and this one is no exception.

Following is a list of career ideas related in one way or another to the government and public service sectors. This list is included here for two reasons. First, to illustrate some unique ways to blend your interests with opportunities. Second, to keep you thinking beyond the obvious.

As you peruse the list you're sure to encounter some occupations you've never heard of before. Good. We hope you get curious enough to look them up. Others may trigger one of those "aha" moments where everything clicks and you know you're onto something good. Either way we hope it helps point the way toward some rewarding opportunities in government and public service.

Ambassador

Armor Officer

Assessor

Aviation Safety Officer

Bank Examiner

Border Inspector

Cabinet-Level Secretary

Census Clerk

Chief of Staff

Chief of Vital Statistics

City Manager

City Clerk

Code Inspector

Combat Aircraft Crew

Combat Aircraft Pilot

Combat Engineer

Combat Operations Officer

Commissioner

Consular Officer

Counterintelligence Agent

Court Clerk

Diplomatic Courier

Economic Officer

Electronic Warfare
Operations Officer

Field Officer

Foreign Service Administrator

Foundation Director

Fund-raiser

General Service Officer

Global Imaging
Systems Specialist

Government Affairs Director

Governor

Infantry Field
Artillery Officer

Inspector General

Legislative Aide

Legislative Assistant

Lieutenant Governor

Management Analysis
Officer

Mayor

Military Intelligence Officer

Missile and Space
Systems Officer

Munitions Officer

National Security Advisor

Nonprofit Organization
Executive

Nuclear Weapons Officer

President

Program Administrator

Representative

Senator

Signals Intelligence Officer

Special Forces Officer

Staff Officer

Submarine Officer

Surface Ship Warfare Officer

Tax Attorney

Tax Auditor

Tax Policy Analyst

Vice President

Big Question #6: are you on the right path?

You've covered a lot of ground so far. You've had a chance to discover more about your own potential and expectations. You've taken some time to explore the realities of a wide variety of career opportunities within this industry.

Now is a good time to sort through all the details and figure out what all this means to you. This process involves equal measures of input from your head and your heart. Be honest, think big, and, most of all, stay true to you.

You may be considering an occupation that requires years of advanced schooling which, from your point of view, seems an insurmountable hurdle. What do you do? Give up before you even get started? We hope not. We'd suggest that you try some creative thinking.

Big Activity #6:
are you on the right path?

Start by asking yourself if you want to pursue this particular career so
badly that you're willing to do whatever it takes to make it. Then stretch
your thinking a little to consider alternative routes, nontraditional career
paths, and other equally meaningful occupations.

Following are some prompts to help you sort through your ideas.
Simply jot down each prompt on a separate sheet of notebook paper and
leave plenty of space for your responses.

Big Activity #6: **are you on the right path?**

One thing I know for sure about my future occupation is

I'd prefer to pursue a career that offers

I'd prefer to pursue a career that requires

A career option I'm now considering is

What appeals to me most about this career is

What concerns me most about this career is

Things that I still need to learn about this career include

Big Activity #6: **are you on the right path?**

Another career option I'm considering is

What appeals to me most about this career is

What concerns me most about this career is

Things that I still need to learn about this career include

Of these two career options I've named, the one that best fits most of my interests, skills, values, and work personality is   because

At this point in the process, I am

❑ Pretty sure I'm on the right track

❑ Not quite sure yet but still interested in exploring some more

❑ Completely clueless about what I want to do

experiment with success

Right about now you may find it encouraging to learn that the average person changes careers five to seven times in his or her life. Plus, most college students change majors several times. Even people who are totally set on what they want to do often end up being happier doing something just a little bit different from what they first imagined.

So, whether you think you've found the ultimate answer to career happiness or you're just as confused as ever, you're in good company. The best advice for navigating these important life choices is this: Always keep the door open to new ideas.

As smart and dedicated as you may be, you just can't predict the future. Some of the most successful professionals in any imaginable field could never ever have predicted what—and how—they would be doing what they actually do today. Why? Because when they were in high school those jobs didn't even exist. It was not too long ago that there were no such things as personal computers, Internet research, digital cameras, mass e-mails, cell phones, or any of the other newfangled tools that are so critical to so many jobs today.

Keeping the door open means being open to recognizing changes in yourself as you mature and being open to changes in the way the world works. It also involves a certain willingness to learn new things and tackle new challenges.

It's easy to see how being open to change can sometimes allow you to go further in your chosen career than you ever dreamed. For instance, in almost any profession you can imagine, technology has fueled unprecedented opportunities. Those people and companies who have embraced this "new way of working" have often surpassed their original expectations of success. Just ask Bill Gates. He's now one of the world's wealthiest men thanks to a company called Microsoft that he cofounded while still a student at Harvard University.

It's a little harder to see, but being open to change can also mean that you may have to let go of your first dream and find a more appropriate one. Maybe your dream is to become a professional athlete. At this point in your life you may think that there's nothing in the world that would possibly make you happier. Maybe you're right and maybe you have the talent and persistence (and the lucky breaks) to take you all the way.

But maybe you don't. Perhaps if you opened yourself to new ideas you'd discover that the best career involves blending your interest in sports with your talent in writing to become a sports journalist or sports information director. Maybe your love of a particular sport and your interest in working with children might best be served in a coaching career. Who knows what you might achieve when you open yourself to all the possibilities?

So, whether you've settled on a career direction or you are still not sure where you want to go, there are several "next steps" to consider. In this section, you'll find three more Big Questions to help keep your career planning moving forward. These Big Questions are:

? Big Question #7: **who knows what you need to know?**

? Big Question #8: **how can you find out what a career is really like?**

? Big Question #9: **how do you know when you've made the right choice?**

Big Question #7:
who knows what you need to know?

When it comes to the nitty-gritty details about what a particular job is really like, who knows what you need to know? Someone with a job like the one you want, of course. They'll have the inside scoop—important information you may never find in books or websites. So make talking to as many people as you can part of your career planning process.

Learn from them how they turned their own challenges into opportunities, how they got started, and how they made it to where they are now. Ask the questions that aren't covered in "official" resources, such as what it is really like to do their job, how they manage to do a good job and have a great life, how they learned what they needed to learn to do their job well, and the best companies or situations to start in.

A good place to start with these career chats or "informational interviews" is with people you know—or more likely, people you know who know people with jobs you find interesting. People you already know include your parents (of course), relatives, neighbors, friends' parents, people who belong to your place of worship or club, and so on.

All it takes to get the process going is gathering up all your nerve and asking these people for help. You'll find that nine and a half times out of 10, the people you encounter will be delighted to help, either by providing information about their careers or by introducing you to people they know who can help.

hints and tips for a successful interview

● TIP #1

Think about your goals for the interview, and write them down.

Be clear about what you want to know after the interview that you didn't know before it.

Remember that the questions for all personal interviews are not the same. You would probably use different questions to write a biography of the person, to evaluate him or her for a job, to do a history of the industry, or to learn about careers that might interest you.

Writing down your objectives will help you stay focused.

● TIP #2

Pay attention to how you phrase your questions.

Some questions that we ask people are "closed" questions; we are looking for a clear answer, not an elaboration. "What time does the movie start?" is a good example of a closed question.

Sometimes, when we ask a closed question, we shortchange ourselves. Think about the difference between "What times are the showings tonight?" and "Is there a 9 P.M. showing?" By asking the second question, you may not find out if there is an 8:45 or 9:30 show.

That can be frustrating. It usually seems so obvious when we ask a question that we expect a full answer. It's important to remember, though, that the person hearing the question doesn't always have the same priorities or know why the question is being asked.

The best example of this? Think of the toddler who answers the phone. When the caller asks, "Is your mom home?" the toddler says, "Yes" and promptly hangs up. Did the child answer the question? As far as he's concerned, he did a great job!

Another problem with closed questions is that they sometimes require so many follow-up questions that the person being interviewed feels like a suspect in an interrogation room.

A series of closed questions may go this way:

Q: What is your job title?
A: Assistant Producer
Q: How long have you had that title?
A: About two years.

Q: What was your title before that?
Q: How long did you have that title?
Q: What is the difference between the two jobs?
Q: What did you do before that?
Q: Where did you learn to do this job?
Q: How did you advance from one job to the next?

An alternative, "open" question invites conversation. An open-question interview might begin this way:

I understand you are an Assistant Producer. I'm really interested in what that job is all about and how you got to be at the level you are today.

Open questions often begin with words like:

Tell me about . . .
How do you feel about . . .
What was it like . . .

● TIP #3

Make the person feel comfortable answering truthfully.

In general, people don't want to say things that they think will make them look bad. How to get at the truth? Be empathic, and make their answers seem "normal."

Ask a performer or artist how he or she feels about getting a bad review from the critics, and you are unlikely to hear, "It really hurts. Sometimes I just want to cry and get out of the business." Or "Critics are so stupid. They never understand what I am trying to do."

Try this approach instead: "So many people in your industry find it hard to deal with the hurt of a bad critical review. How do you handle it when that happens?"

ask the experts

You can learn a lot by interviewing people who are already successful in the types of careers you're interested in. In fact, we followed our own advice and interviewed several people who have been successful in the fields of government and public service to share with you here.

Before you get started on your own interview, take a few minutes to look through the results of some of ours. To make it easier for you to compare the responses of all the people we interviewed, we have presented our interviews as a panel discussion that reveals important success lessons these people have learned along the way. Each panelist is introduced on the next two pages.

Our interviewees gave us great information about things like what their jobs are really like, how they got to where they are, and even provided a bit of sage advice for people like you who are just getting started.

So Glad You Asked

In addition to the questions we asked in the interviews in this book, you might want to add some of these questions to your own interviews:

- How did your childhood interests relate to your choice of career path?
- How did you first learn about the job you have today?
- In what ways is your job different from how you expected it to be?
- Tell me about the parts of your job that you really like.
- If you could get someone to take over part of your job for you, what aspect would you most like to give up?
- If anything were possible, how would you change your job description?
- What kinds of people do you usually meet in your work?
- Walk me through the whole process of getting your type of product made and distributed. Tell me about all the people who are involved.
- Tell me about the changes you have seen in your industry over the years. What do you see as the future of the industry?
- Are there things you would do differently in your career if you could do it all over?

real people with real jobs in government and public service

Following are introductions to our panel of experts. Get acquainted with their backgrounds and then use their job titles to track their stories throughout the eight success lessons.

- **Bill Atkinson** is **Deputy Chief** of the General Officer Management Office for the U.S. Army and works at the Pentagon.
- **Dr. Michael Brintnall** is Executive Director of the American Political Science Association in Washington, D.C. (His interview comments are designated as **Executive Director 1** in the following section.)
- **Kimberly Green** is Executive Director of the National Association of State Directors of Career Technical Education Consortium, a non-profit organization based in Washington, D.C. (Her interview comments are designated as **Executive Director 2** in the following section.)
- **Dr. Thomas Olson** is an **Agricultural Development Officer** for the U.S. Agency for International Development.
- **Robert Rauf** is **IT** (information technology) **Director** for the North Carolina State Board of Elections.
- **Jim Wagner** works in places all over the world with the U.S. Department of State as a **Foreign Service Officer**.

Bill Atkinson

Dr. Michael Brintnall

Kimberly Green

Jim Wagner

Everybody has to start some-where!

Following is a list of first jobs once held by our esteemed panel of experts.

Assembly line worker

Baby-sitter

Brick loader

Dairy farm worker

Farmer

Musician

Paperboy

Retail store manager

Security guard

Short-order cook

Surveyor's helper

Success Lesson #1:
Work is a good thing when you find the right career.

- **Tell us what it's like to work in your current career.**

    Agricultural Development Officer: I represent the United States in helping developing nations to become more productive and prosperous.

    Deputy Chief: I help support the Army Chief of Staff on all general officer management matters to include accessions, assignments, retirements, force structure and requirements, promotions, joint duty, acquisition, professional development and training, reserve components, and personnel actions. I also supervise and coordinate the day-to-day operations of all officers and soldiers assigned to the General Officer Management Office (GOMO), and coordinate daily with other Army staff agencies, including the Office of the Secretary of Defense.

    Executive Director 1: I direct a nonprofit association of professors and other people who study political science. Our association helps professors carry out their research into how government and politics works. We publish their studies, and we encourage them to be better teachers and scholars. The association itself is like running a small business, but the product is helping professionals do their jobs better, not making things to sell.

    Executive Director 2: I work with Congress and the administration to make sure there is adequate funding and appropriate policies in place to support high school and community college career technical education programs.

    Foreign Service Officer: I promote those things that make us uniquely Americans—democracy, respect for diversity, economic opportunities—in our relations with other countries and other peoples around the world.

    IT Director: I manage the support of the computers and software used by the state and county elections offices in North Carolina.

Success Lesson #2:
One thing leads to another along any career path.

- **How did you end up doing what you're doing now?**

    Agricultural Development Officer: After I received my master's degree I got a job with the U.S. government in Washington,

D.C. It was a career-track position as an economist. After nearly one year I was offered a short-term position to work on a World Bank-funded study in Thailand, so I quit my job in Washington. My colleagues simply could not believe what I was doing!

Deputy Chief: I entered the Army, as an officer, right out of college (West Point). I found that I enjoyed being a soldier and working with soldiers, so I made the Army a career (22+ years). I found that I was particularly drawn to service to the nation. When I retired from the military, I decided that I wanted to continue to serve the country and work with soldiers. Fortunately, the Army was in the process of converting the last job that I had from a military one to a civilian one. I applied, interviewed, and competed with other applicants for the job; obviously, I was hired.

Executive Director 2: I began my studies in political science as most do—on the law school track. However, I felt that I was learning about the history of politics rather than skills that would help me be an effective attorney. I changed majors to industrial and labor relations—it was the best move I made. Not only did I learn negotiating skills, strengthen my analytical skills, and broaden my education by learning about organizational behavior and the politics of business and labor, but I also got an internship.

This internship tied together what I learning in college and gave me a chance to begin to explore policy work. That internship led to my first job out of college as a government relations staff person. I then moved up to be deputy executive director which led to my current position.

Executive Director 1: After I started to study for a career in city planning, I decided that I liked the idea of teaching others and doing research about how to change things for the better. After teaching for a while I realized that what I liked best was helping other people to be good professors and researchers.

Foreign Service Officer: I was heavily involved in music performance and played with several bands and orchestras as a teen. The Foreign Service looks for people with varied backgrounds and something "different" (like a heavy music education) adds to your attraction for the Service. In college and graduate school, I sought jobs in government—the Ohio Legislative Budget Office, the U.S. Library of Congress—to give a wide exposure to public service possibilities.

IT Director: When I started working in programming I liked programming and really didn't want to be a manager. As I got some experience as a manager, I realized that I could make a bigger contribution and have a greater impact by directing many people's activities.

I worked for IBM for almost 30 years. Most of that time was spent managing the development of new software products. This management experience and training helped me at IBM and in other jobs since then. I have moved several times in my career for better opportunities. This has always been difficult and has to be balanced with family responsibilities.

Success Lesson #3:
Career goals change and so do you.

- ## When you were in high school, what career did you hope to pursue?

Agricultural Development Officer: Prior to college I had no idea what I wanted to do.

Executive Director 2: My current career has nothing to do with my childhood visions of being a veterinarian.

Deputy Chief: I always thought that I would go into the corporate world and make a huge salary.

Executive Director 1: As a teenager, I wanted a career where I would work to make the community better, like being a city planner.

Foreign Service Officer: I always wanted a career that would expose me to other cultures, places, and people. A foreign service career is the perfect place for a person who has a grand curiosity about the world beyond. I started with the notion that I would be a linguist and work as an interpreter or translator. (They are different—the interpreter works with verbal communication; the translator works with the written word.) But I knew enough about myself to realize that I didn't want to facilitate the conversation; I wanted to be part of the conversation. The Foreign Service combines a dedication to public service with an intellectual curiosity about the world.

IT Director: When I was a teenager I thought I wanted to be a civil engineer.

- ## What was it that made you change directions?

Agricultural Development Officer: After college I joined the Peace Corps, and it was then that I decided that living and working overseas in development would be both challenging and fulfilling.

Deputy Chief: I entered the Army, in large part, because my father was an Army officer. His love of the Army had a big influence on me.

Executive Director 2: I began college with the dream of going to law school.

Executive Director 1: I thought my career would be a straight path—I'd learn one skill, such as city planning or being a college professor, and stay with that forever. What happened is that instead I moved from one kind of work to another—university, government, college, nonprofit association, etc. The ideas and motivations all stayed the same, but the jobs were different.

IT Director: When I worked as a surveyor while going to college I found out that civil engineers spend a lot of time outside in the summer heat and the winter cold. At the same time I started working as a computer operator and saw what programmers do and how interesting it was. This made me move in that direction.

I started working as a computer operator and then as a programmer before going into management. Understanding what the people that work for you have to do is an important part of knowing how to manage them.

Success Lesson #4:
There's more than one way to get an education.

- **Where did you learn the skills of your field, both formally (school) and informally (experience)?**

    Agricultural Development Officer: Optimism cannot be taught and it is really useful in this business. As Yogi Berra said, "you can observe a lot just by watching," and "just watching" is a useful skill in a new country. Sometimes it is necessary to drink tea for a few hours before even bringing up the real reason for your visit. Sometimes a situation will arise that can make or break a project. Lots of things are simply trial and error. This is not an exact science, yet we are learning more every day and the literature is improving all the time.

Deputy Chief: My entire Army career helped prepare me for my current job, as I now have a good idea of what Army generals do and what the Army needs. I have been in this office for eight years now and have a very good background and familiarity with most aspects of general officer management.

One trait that I have noticed when observing a mentor, or someone who I respect, is that it is important to treat people well. I have seen generals talk to young soldiers in a very sincere, caring, and courteous manner. And it's genuine. Good leaders take care of their people. Sometimes it means having to reprimand them. But it always means treating them with respect. If you take care of your people and show them that you care about them, they will appreciate it and will return the sentiment.

Executive Director 2: Much of my current work was adapted knowledge. I learned the basics in my degree program—analytical skills and communication skills. Applying all of these skills in the context of an association and in the context of a policy environment has all been learned through experience. What I have learned is that a positive work ethic, honesty, and integrity are key no matter what type of work you do.

I also strongly believe that advocates must passionately believe in the cause or issue they represent. Many times when I give a presentation, members of the audience say to me "you must really believe in what you do" or "you must really like your job." And I say, "yes." I can't imagine being effective, let alone happy, working for an issue or cause you don't believe in. Life is too short!

Executive Director 1: The simplest thing I learned "on the job" was how to write. My first boss would take my reports, and sit down with me and a red pencil and go through it line by line. It wasn't long before I learned to write concisely, clearly, and quickly.

Other times, in the government, I would observe different managers: some would include lots of people in their discussions, listen to everyone, ask questions, then quiet the room down, think a bit, and make a decision. I can't say I've learned how to do that very well, but I certainly learned what to aspire to.

Foreign Service Officer: A foreign language can only be truly learned through practice. Book and classroom learning provides the fundamentals; practice puts it all into place. My first foreign service assignment was to Sandinista-controlled Nicaragua. During my two years there, I was stopped on the street by every security force possible—from a lone soldier patrolling a deserted street late at night to an immigration officer checking for migration documents in a busy supermarket parking lot. That is where I turned my classroom Spanish into a functional skill!

Also, adaptability is both a skill and a trait that must be cultivated to succeed in this type of work. Moving jobs every two or three years and going to foreign locales and representing the United States to foreign governments requires you to adapt every day to a new work environment, a new set of problems. If nothing else, the work isn't boring!

IT Director: The biggest challenge in this work is learning how to successfully manage people to accomplish a job. A lot of management classes can give you clues about what to do, but each situation is different and you can only get good at this through experience.

Success Lesson #5:
Every career has its ups and downs.

- **What aspect of your work do you most enjoy?**

Agricultural Development Officer: I really enjoy living and working overseas in different cultures and with different types of people. We in the West really do have the technology and the expertise to improve the lives of the developing nations tremendously. Sometimes a very simple solution can have a tremendous impact and it is great to see the results.

Deputy Chief: There are several aspects to my work that I particularly enjoy, including working with soldiers, serving the Army and the nation, being an advisor and confidant to Army generals (one-, two-, three-, and four-star), and feeling like what I do makes a difference. It's also exciting to occasionally meet military "big wheels" like the Secretary of the Army and Chief of Staff of the Army. For the most part, they are very personable and very impressive.

Executive Director 2: It sounds like a cliché, but I really enjoy that the work that I do contributes positively to our country. I also enjoy the variety of my work and the many people I get to meet (from students and parents to business and political leaders).

Executive Director 1: I like three things about my job a lot. One is that the goal of the job is really important—improving what we know about how government and politics work and how to improve them. Another is the pace of activities every day—there is always something different going on. Sometimes the work is intellectual, such as talking with professors. And sometimes the work gets very practical, like figuring out how to make the heating system work in the building. And finally I like the people I work with. There are

25 of us—big enough to have lots of different projects going on yet small enough to be a friendly little community.

Foreign Service Officer: Change. We are assigned to a job for two or three years and then move on to another job, usually in another geographic location. This is the ideal job for the person with habitual wanderlust.

IT Director: Helping to create new solutions that make people's jobs easier and more productive is one aspect that is very rewarding. The other is giving guidance to employees that helps them advance their careers.

- **What aspect of your work do you least enjoy?**

  Agricultural Development Officer: Unfortunately much of my work is with and through governments, including the U.S. government, and many good things are sacrificed for the sake of "politics."

  Deputy Chief: The hours are terrible (6 A.M. to 6 P.M.). But I don't travel for work and I rarely work on weekends.

  Executive Director 2: The hours are certainly not regular.

  Executive Director 1: Working in an association, there are lots of different members voicing opinions and needs and lots of different directions that the association's leaders would like to go. Sometimes those needs are difficult to respond to and the decision making takes a long time with a lot of disagreements.

  Foreign Service Officer: The State Department is a bureaucracy and an organization with the demands and needs of any large organization. Having to worry about a broken photocopier might seem trivial if you are negotiating a peace treaty, but the photocopier is vital to the organization and must be fixed.

  IT Director: The most difficult job as a manager comes when you have to fire someone when they are not performing. With experience you begin to understand it as necessary for the success of an organization but it's still tough to do on a personal level.

Success Lesson #6:
Good choices and hard work are a potent combination.

● **What are you most proud of in your career?**

Agricultural Development Officer: My juices start flowing when I can see a high government official in a developing nation begin to understand that markets can work—that Western technology can solve many problems and that he or she can change a policy or a regulation to make it work for the betterment of the people in general.

Deputy Chief: In my current job, I would say that it is very satisfying any time we are able to successfully move an action through the Pentagon (from the Army to the Joint Staff to the Secretary of Defense) so that it can go to the president or Congress for a decision. There is a lot of hard work that goes into preparing the final product and putting it together so that the president and members of Congress are confident that they are making a wise and well-informed decision.

Executive Director 2: I would have to say when the first piece of legislation that I worked on was signed by the president was a very proud day for me. All the hard work paid off. And the positive impact the legislation would have for students in every state of the union was very rewarding.

Executive Director 1: Completing my own research projects has always been fun and I like that best when my studies are directly helping to improve a community or a program. I've also valued the chance to work internationally and to build partnerships with people with similar interests in other countries.

Foreign Service Officer: Convincing both Washington and our governmental counterparts in European Union capitals that we needed to embark on a new means of cooperation in the investigation and prosecution of international crime and terrorism. Prior to 9/11, enhanced cooperation was a "theory"; post-9/11, it was the imperative. My work aided in the signing of new extradition and mutual legal assistance treaties with the European Union.

IT Director: I have managed the development of new software several times in my career. The most rewarding part is when you see these projects through from their inception to the completion.

Success Lesson #7:
You can learn from other people's mistakes.

● **Is there anything you wish you had done differently?**

Deputy Chief: As I said earlier, I thought I was bound for a corporate life. I did not intend to make the Army a career. But my military experience and assignments were exactly what I needed to make me successful in this job.

Executive Director 2: Not really.

Executive Director 1: I can imagine doing a lot differently—even being a physicist instead of a political scientist. But that is not regret; it just would have been a different path. I do wish I'd mastered some foreign languages early on.

Foreign Service Officer: I probably would have sought a geographic or functional specialization earlier on in my career. I'm considered a generalist, which means I should be able to "do everything, anywhere"; in reality, sticking with and perfecting one or two specialties makes you more marketable as you advance in career tracks.

Agricultural Development Officer: I made the mistake of getting a Ph.D. before I joined USAID. This is not necessarily the key to bureaucratic success or "climbing the ladder." A simple college degree and some experience overseas can suffice. Peace Corps is excellent although many other programs exist these days that can provide similar or even more important experience.

USAID has an entry-level program specifically for young college graduates. It is highly competitive, although if you read the website and prepare you will greatly enhance your probability of being selected.

Success Lesson #8:
A little advice goes a long way.

- ## What advice do you have for a young person just getting started?

Agricultural Development Officer: First get a college degree. Second, read authors who write about international development, such as Bill Easterly, Mancur Olson (deceased), C.K. Prahalad, and Hernando de Soto, as well as the annual World Bank Report (*www.worldbank.org/annualreport*) on the status of emerging countries. Third, read the United States Agency for International Development website (*www.usaid.gov*), particularly when you apply for the International Development Intern Program.

Actually getting a job like mine requires three additional things. First, a technical skill is necessary in USAID—be it in agriculture, health, environment, water and waste-water management, or urban planning. Second, a good sense of what has made western markets successful is also handy. Third, patience, diplomacy, and lots of persistence really pay off in the long run.

Deputy Chief: First, find something that you enjoy and that you are good at. If you have a job or career in which you are happy, satisfied, and productive, you have a great combination.

Second, set goals, but be willing to rethink your goals from time to time. If necessary, adjust your goals. There is nothing wrong with this. People change over time. So do their desires. It is very wise to have goals (most people don't), to check them every once in awhile, adjust, and continue to pursue them—it's a process.

Third, whatever you do, be the best that you can. Be a student of your profession. I have learned so much through experience but I have also learned a lot by doing good research. Don't ever get lax: always study and become more informed.

And last, enjoy the journey and don't be surprised where it might take you. My Army career and my current career were nowhere in my plans when I was a teenager. But I kept setting, evaluating, resetting, and working toward my goals. I am glad that I did and I am happy where it has taken me so far.

Executive Director 2: Intern in a congressional office or for an association. This will expose you to the pace of work, types of work to be done, and the environment you would work in.

Big Activity #7:
who knows what you need to know?

It's one thing to read about conducting an informational interview, but it's another thing altogether to actually do one. Now it's your turn to shine. Just follow these steps for doing it like a pro!

Step 1: Identify the people you want to talk to about their work.

Step 2: Set up a convenient time to meet in person or talk over the phone.

Step 3: Make up a list of questions that reflect things you'd really like to know about that person's work. Go for the open questions you just read about.

Step 4: Talk away! Take notes as your interviewee responds to each question.

Step 5: Use your notes to write up a "news" article that describes the person and his or her work.

Step 6: Place all your notes and the finished "news" article in your Big Question AnswerBook.

Big Activity #7: **who knows what you need to know?**

contact information	appointments/sample questions
name	day time
company	location
title	
address	
	sample questions:
phone	
email	
name	day time
company	location
title	
address	
	sample questions:
phone	
email	
name	day time
company	location
title	
address	
	sample questions:
phone	
email	

CONTACT INFO

Big Activity #7: who knows what you need to know?

questions	answers

INTERVIEW NOTES

Big Activity #7: **who knows what you need to know?**

questions	answers

INTERVIEW NOTES

Big Activity #7: **who knows what you need to know?**

NEWS

Big Activity #7: who knows what you need to know?

NEWS

Big Question #8:

how can you find out what a career is really like?

There are some things you just have to figure out for yourself. Things like whether your interest in pursuing a career in marine biology is practical if you plan to live near the Mojave Desert.

Other things you have to see for yourself. Words are sometimes not enough when it comes to conveying what a job is really like on a day-to-day basis—what it looks like, sounds like, and feels like.

Here are a few ideas for conducting an on-the-job reality check.

identify typical types of workplaces

Think of all the places that jobs like the ones you like take place. Almost all of the careers in this book, or ones very similar to them, exist in the corporate world, in the public sector, and in the military. And don't forget the option of going into business for yourself!

For example: Are you interested in public relations? You can find a place for yourself in almost any sector of our economy. Of course, companies definitely want to promote their products. But don't limit yourself to the Fortune 500 corporate world. Hospitals, schools, and manufacturers need your services. Cities, states, and even countries also need your services. They want to increase tourism, get businesses to relocate there, and convince workers to live there or students to study there. Each military branch needs to recruit new members and to show how they are using the money they receive from the government for medical research, taking care of families, and other non-news-breaking uses. Charities, community organizations, and even religious groups want to promote the good things they are doing so that they will get more members, volunteers, contributions, and funding. Political candidates, parties, and special interest groups all want to promote their messages. Even actors, dancers, and writers need to promote themselves.

Not interested in public relations but know you want a career that involves lots of writing? You've thought about becoming the more obvious choices—novelist, newspaper reporter, or English teacher. But you don't want to overlook other interesting possibilities, do you?

What if you also enjoy technical challenges? Someone has to write the documentation for all those computer games and software.

Love cars? Someone has to write those owner's manuals too.

Ditto on those government reports about safety and environmental standards for industries.

Maybe community service is your thing. You can mix your love for helping people with writing grant proposals seeking funds for programs at hospitals, day care centers, or rehab centers.

Talented in art and design? Those graphics you see in magazine advertisements, on your shampoo bottle, and on a box of cereal all have to be created by someone.

That someone could be you.

find out about the job outlook

Organizations like the U.S. Bureau of Labor Statistics spend a lot of time and energy gathering data on what kinds of jobs are most in demand now and what kinds are projected to be in demand in the future. Find out what the job outlook is for a career you like. A good resource for this data can be found on-line at America's Career InfoNet at *www.acinet.org/acinet.*

This information will help you understand whether the career options you find most appealing are viable. In other words, job outlook data will give you a better sense of your chances of actually finding gainful employment in your chosen profession—a rather important consideration from any standpoint.

Be realistic. You may really, really want to be a film critic at a major newspaper. Maybe your ambition is to become the next Roger Ebert.

Think about this. How many major newspapers are there? Is it reasonable to pin all your career hopes on a job for which there are only about 10 positions in the whole country? That doesn't mean that it's impossible to achieve your ambition. After all, someone has to fill those positions. It should just temper your plans with realism and perhaps encourage you to have a back-up plan, just in case.

look at training requirements

Understand what it takes to prepare yourself for a specific job. Some jobs require only a high school diploma. Others require a couple of years of technical training, while still others require four years or more in college.

Be sure to investigate a variety of training options. Look at training programs and colleges you may like to attend. Check out their websites to see what courses are required for the major you want. Make sure you're willing to "do the time" in school to prepare yourself for a particular occupation.

see for yourself

There's nothing quite like seeing for yourself what a job is like. Talk with a teacher or guidance counselor to arrange a job-shadowing opportunity with someone who is in the job or in a similar one.

Job shadowing is an activity that involves actually spending time at work with someone to see what a particular job is like up close and personal. It's an increasingly popular option and your school may participate in specially designated job-shadowing days. For some especially informative resources on job shadowing, visit *www.jobshadow.org*.

Another way to test-drive different careers is to find summer jobs and internships that are similar to the career you hope to pursue.

make a Plan B

Think of the alternatives! Often it's not possible to have a full-time job in the field you love. Some jobs just don't pay enough to meet the needs of every person or family. Maybe you recognize that you don't have the talent, drive, or commitment to rise to the top. Or, perhaps you can't afford the years of work it takes to get established or you place a higher priority on spending time with family than that career might allow.

If you can see yourself in any of those categories, DO NOT GIVE UP on what you love! There is always more than one way to live out your dreams. Look at some of the other possibilities in this book. Find a way to integrate your passion into other jobs or your free time.

Lots of people manage to accomplish this in some fairly impressive ways. For instance, the Knicks City Dancers, known for their incredible performances and for pumping up the crowd at Knicks basketball games, include an environmental engineer, a TV news assignment editor, and a premed student, in addition to professional dancers. The Broadband Pickers, a North Texas bluegrass band, is made up of five lawyers and one businessman. In fact, even people who are extremely successful in a field that they love find ways to indulge their other passions. Paul Newman, the actor and director, not only drives race cars as a hobby, but also produces a line of gourmet foods and donates the profits to charity.

Get the picture? Good. Hang in there and keep moving forward in your quest to find your way toward a great future.

Big Activity #8:
how can you find out what a career is really like?

This activity will help you conduct a reality check about your future career in two ways. First, it prompts you to find out more about the nitty-gritty details you really need to know to make a well-informed career choice. Second, it helps you identify strategies for getting a firsthand look at what it's like to work in a given profession—day in and day out.

Here's how to get started:

Step 1: Write the name of the career you're considering at the top of a sheet of paper (or use the following worksheets if this is your book).

Step 2: Create a checklist (or, if this is your book, use the one provided on the following pages) covering two types of reality-check items.

First, list four types of information to investigate:
- training requirements
- typical workplaces
- job outlook
- similar occupations

Second, list three types of opportunities to pursue:
- job shadowing
- apprenticeship
- internship

Step 3: Use resources such as America's Career InfoNet at *www.acinet.org* and Career OneStop at *www.careeronestop.org* to seek out the information you need.

Step 4: Make an appointment with your school guidance counselor to discuss how to pursue hands-on opportunities to learn more about this occupation. Use the space provided on the following worksheets to jot down preliminary contact information and a brief summary of why or why not each career is right for you.

Step 5: When you're finished, place these notes in your Big Question AnswerBook.

Big Activity #8: **how can you find out what a career is really like?**

career choice:	
training requirements	
typical workplaces	
job outlook	
similar occupations	

INFORMATION

Big Activity #8: how can you find out what a career is really like?

job shadowing	when: where: who: observations and impressions:
apprenticeship	when: where: who: observations and impressions:
internship	when: where: who: observations and impressions:

OPPORTUNITIES

Big Question #9:

how do you know when you've made the right choice?

When it comes right down to it, finding the career that's right for you is like shopping in a mall with 12,000 different stores. Finding the right fit may require trying on lots of different options.

All the Big Questions you've answered so far have been designed to expand your career horizons and help you clarify what you really want in a career. The next step is to see how well you've managed to integrate your interests, capabilities, goals, and ambitions with the realities of specific opportunities.

There are two things for you to keep in mind as you do this.

First, recognize the value of all the hard work you did to get to this point. If you've already completed the first eight activities thoughtfully and honestly, whatever choices you make will be based on solid knowledge about yourself and your options. You've learned to use a process that works just as well now, when you're trying to get an inkling of what you want to do with your life, as it will later when you have solid job offers on the table and need to make decisions that will affect your life and family.

Second, always remember that sometimes, even when you do everything right, things don't turn out the way you'd planned. That's called life. It happens. And it's not the end of the world. Even if you make what seems to be a bad choice, know this—there's no such thing as a wasted experience. The paths you take, the training you receive, the people you meet—they ultimately fall together like puzzle pieces to make you who you are and prepare you for what you're meant to do.

That said, here's a strategy to help you confirm that you are making the very best choices you can.

Big Activity #9:
how do you know when you've made the right choice?

One way to confirm that the choices you are making are right for you is to look at both sides of this proverbial coin: what you are looking for and what each career offers. The following activity will help you think this through.

Step 1: To get started, make two charts with four columns (or, if this is your book, use the following worksheets).

Step 2: Label the first column of the first chart as "Yes Please!" Under this heading list all the qualities you absolutely must have in a future job. This might include factors such as the kind of training you'd prefer to pursue (college, apprenticeship, etc.); the type of place where you'd like to work (big office, high-tech lab, in the great outdoors, etc.); and the sorts of people you want to work with (children, adults, people with certain needs, etc.). It may also include salary requirements or dress code preferences.

Step 3: Now at the top of the next three columns write the names of three careers you are considering. (This is a little like Big Activity #3 where you examined your work values. But now you know a lot more and you're ready to zero in on specific careers.)

Step 4: Go down the list and use an *X* to indicate careers that do indeed feature the desired preferences. Use an *O* to indicate those that do not.

Step 5: Tally up the number of *Xs* and *Os* at the bottom of each career column to find out which comes closest to your ideal job.

Step 6: In the first column of the second chart add a heading called "No Thanks!" This is where you'll record the factors you simply prefer not to deal with. Maybe long hours, physically demanding work, or jobs that require years of advanced training just don't cut it for you. Remember that part of figuring out what you do want to do involves understanding what you don't want to do.

Step 7: Repeat steps 2 through 5 for these avoid-at-all-costs preferences as you did for the must-have preferences above.

Big Activity #9: **how do you know when you've made the right choice?**

yes please!	career #1	career #2	career #3
totals	__X__O	__X__O	__X__O

Big Activity #9: **how do you know when you've made the right choice?**

no thanks!	career #1	career #2	career #3
totals	__X__O	__X__O	__X__O

? Big Question #10:
what's next?

Think of this experience as time well invested in your future. And expect it to pay off in a big way down the road. By now, you have worked (and perhaps wrestled) your way through nine important questions:

- ? Big Question #1: **who are you?**
- ? Big Question #2: **what are your interests and strengths?**
- ? Big Question #3: **what are your work values?**
- ? Big Question #4: **what is your work personality?**
- ? Big Question #5: **do you have the right skills?**
- ? Big Question #6: **are you on the right path?**
- ? Big Question #7: **who knows what you need to know?**
- ? Big Question #8: **how can you find out what a career is really like?**
- ? Big Question #9: **how do you know when you've made the right choice?**

But what if you still don't have a clue about what you want to do with your life?

Don't worry. You're talking about one of the biggest life decisions you'll ever make. These things take time.

It's okay if you don't have all the definitive answers yet. At least you do know how to go about finding them. The process you've used to work through this book is one that you can rely on throughout your life to help you sort through the options and make sound career decisions.

So what's next?

More discoveries, more exploration, and more experimenting with success are what come next. Keep at it and you're sure to find your way to wherever your dreams and ambitions lead you.

And, just for good measure, here's one more Big Activity to help point you in the right direction.

List five things you can do to move forward in your career planning process (use a separate sheet if you need to). Your list may include tasks such as talking to your guidance counselor about resources your school makes available, checking out colleges or other types of training programs that can prepare you for your life's work, or finding out about job-shadowing or internship opportunities in your community. Remember to include any appropriate suggestions from the Get Started Now! list included with each career profile in Section 2 of this book.

Big Activity #10: **what's next?**

career planning to-do list

1

2

3

4

5

a final word

You are now officially equipped with the tools you need to track down a personally appropriate profession any time you have the need or desire. You've discovered more about who you are and what you want. You've explored a variety of career options within a very important industry. You've even taken it upon yourself to experiment with what it might be like to actually work in certain occupations.

Now it's up to you to put all this newfound knowledge to work for you. While you're at it, here's one more thing to keep in mind: Always remember that there's no such thing as a wasted experience. Certainly some experiences are more positive than others, but they all teach us something.

Chances are you may not get everything right the first time out. It may turn out that you were incorrect about how much you would love to go to a certain college or pursue a particular profession. That doesn't mean you're doomed to failure. It simply means that you've lived and learned. Sometimes you just won't know for sure about one direction or another until you try things out a bit. Nothing about your future has to be written in stone. Allow yourself some freedom to experiment with various options until you find something that really clicks for you.

Figuring out what you want to do with the rest of your life is a big deal. It's probably one of the most exciting and among the most intimidating decisions you'll ever make. It's a decision that warrants clear-headed thought and wholehearted investigation. It's a process that's likely to take you places you never dared imagine if you open yourself up to all the possibilities. Take a chance on yourself and seek out and follow your most valued hopes and dreams into the workplace.

Best wishes for a bright future!

Appendix

a virtual support team

As you continue your quest to determine just what it is you want to do with your life, you'll find that you are not alone. There are many people and organizations who want to help you succeed. Here are two words of advice—let them! Take advantage of all the wonderful resources so readily available to you.

The first place to start is your school's guidance center. There you are quite likely to find a variety of free resources which include information about careers, colleges, and other types of training opportunities; details about interesting events, job shadowing activities, and internship options; and access to useful career assessment tools.

In addition, since you are the very first generation on the face of the earth to have access to a world of information just the click of a mouse away—use it! The following Internet resources provide all kinds of information and ideas that can help you find your future.

make an informed choice

Following are five of the very best career-oriented websites currently on-line. Be sure to bookmark these websites and visit them often as you consider various career options.

America's Career Info Net *www.acinet.org/acinet/default.asp*

Quite possibly the most comprehensive source of career exploration anywhere, this U.S. Department of Labor website includes all kinds of current information about wages, market conditions, employers, and employment trends. Make sure to visit the site's career video library where you'll find links to over 450 videos featuring real people doing real jobs.

Careers & Colleges *www.careersandcolleges.com*

Each year Careers & Colleges publishes four editions of *Careers & Colleges* magazine, designed to help high school students set and meet their academic, career, and financial goals. Ask your guidance counselor about receiving free copies. You'll also want to visit the excellent Careers and Colleges website. Here you'll encounter their "Virtual Guidance Counselor," an interactive career database that allows you to match your interests with college majors or careers that are right for you.

Career Voyages *www.careervoyages.gov*

This website is brought to you compliments of collaboration between the U.S. Department of Labor and the U.S. Department of Education and is designed especially for students like you. Here you'll find information on high-growth, high-demand occupations and the skills and education needed to attain those jobs.

Job Shadow *www.jobshadow.org*

See your future via a variety of on-line virtual job-shadowing videos and interviews featuring people with fascinating jobs.

My Cool Career *www.mycoolcareer.com*

This website touts itself as the "coolest career dream site for teens and 20's." See for yourself as you work your way through a variety of useful self-assessment quizzes, listen to an assortment of on-line career shows, and explore all kinds of career resources.

investigate local opportunities

To get a better understanding of employment happenings in your state, visit these state-specific career information websites.

Alabama
www.ajb.org/al
www.al.plusjobs.com

Alaska
www.jobs.state.ak.us
www.akcis.org/default.htm

Arizona
www.ajb.org/az
www.ade.state.az.us/cte/AZCrn
    project10.asp

Arkansas
www.ajb.org/ar
www.careerwatch.org
www.ioscar.org/ar

California
www.calmis.ca.gov
www.ajb.org/ca
www.eurekanet.org

Colorado
www.coloradocareer.net
www.coworkforce.com/lmi

Connecticut
www1.ctdol.state.ct.us/jcc
www.ctdol.state.ct.us/lmi

Delaware
www.ajb.org/de
www.delewareworks.com

District of Columbia
www.ajb.org/dc
www.dcnetworks.org

Florida
www.Florida.access.bridges.com
www.employflorida.net

Georgia
www.gcic.peachnet.edu
    (Ask your school guidance counselor
    for your school's free password and
    access code)
www.dol.state.ga.us/js

Hawaii
www.ajb.org/hi
www.careerkokua.org

Idaho
www.ajb.org/id
www.cis.idaho.gov

Illinois
www.ajb.org/il
www.ilworkinfo.com

Indiana
www.ajb.org/in
http://icpac.indiana.edu

Iowa
www.ajb.org/ia
www.state.ia.us/iccor

Kansas
www.ajb.org/ks
www.kansasjoblink.com/ada

Kentucky
www.ajb.org/ky

Louisiana
www.ajb.org/la
www.ldol.state.la.us/jobpage.asp

Maine
www.ajb.org/me
www.maine.gov/labor/lmis

Maryland
www.ajb.org/md
www.careernet.state.md.us

Massachusetts
www.ajb.org/ma
http://masscis.intocareers.org

Michigan
www.mois.org

Minnesota
www.ajb.org/mn
www.iseek.org

Mississippi
www.ajb.org/ms
www.mscareernet.org

Missouri
www.ajb.org/mo
www.greathires.org

Montana
www.ajb.org/mt
http://jsd.dli.state.mt.us/mjshome.asp

Nebraska
www.ajb.org/ne
www.careerlink.org

New Hampshire
www.nhes.state.nh.us

New Jersey
www.ajb.org/nj
www.wnjpin.net/coei

New Mexico
www.ajb.org/nm
www.dol.state.nm.us/soicc/upto21.html

Nevada
www.ajb.org/nv
http://nvcis.intocareers.org

New York
www.ajb.org/ny
www.nycareerzone.org

North Carolina
www.ajb.org/nc
www.ncsoicc.org
www.nccareers.org

North Dakota
www.ajb.org/nd
www.imaginend.com
www.ndcrn.com/students

Ohio
www.ajb.org/oh
https://scoti.ohio.gov/scoti_lexs

Oklahoma
www.ajb.org/ok
www.okcareertech.org/guidance
http://okcrn.org

Oregon
www.hsd.k12.or.us/crls

Pennsylvania
www.ajb.org/pa
www.pacareerlink.state.pa.us

Rhode Island
www.ajb.org/ri
www.dlt.ri.gov/lmi/jobseeker.htm

South Carolina
www.ajb.org/sc
www.scois.org/students.htm

South Dakota
www.ajb.org/sd

Tennessee
www.ajb.org/tn
www.tcids.utk.edu

Texas
www.ajb.org/tx
www.ioscar.org/tx
www.cdr.state.tx.us/Hotline/Hotline.html

Utah
www.ajb.org/ut
http://jobs.utah.gov/wi/occi.asp

Vermont
www.ajb.org/vt
www.vermontjoblink.com
www.vtlmi.info/oic.cfm

Virginia
www.ajb.org/va
www.vacrn.net

Washington
www.ajb.org/wa
www.workforceexplorer.com
*www.wa.gov/esd/lmea/soicc/
   sohome.htm*

West Virginia
www.ajb.org/wv
www.state.wv.us/bep/lmi

Wisconsin
www.ajb.org/wi
www.careers4wi.wisc.edu
http://wiscareers.wisc.edu/splash.asp

Wyoming
www.ajb.org/wy
*http://uwadmnweb.uwyo.edu/SEO/
   wcis.htm*

get a job

Whether you're curious about the kinds of jobs currently in big demand or you're actually looking for a job, the following websites are a great place to do some virtual job-hunting.

America's Job Bank *www.ajb.org*

Another example of your (or, more accurately, your parent's) tax dollars at work, this well-organized website is sponsored by the U.S. Department of Labor. Job seekers can post resumes and use the site's search engines to search through over a million job listings by location or by job type.

Monster.com *www.monster.com*

One of the Internet's most widely used employment websites, this is where you can search for specific types of jobs in specific parts of the country, network with millions of people, and find useful career advice.

explore by special interests

An especially effective way to explore career options is to look at careers associated with a personal interest or fascination with a certain type of industry. The following websites help you narrow down your options in a focused way.

What Interests You? *www.bls.gov/k12*
This Bureau of Labor Statistics website provides information about careers associated with 12 special interest areas: math, reading, science, social studies, music and arts, building and fixing things, helping people, computers, law, managing money, sports, and nature.

Construct My Future *www.constructmyfuture.com*
With over $600 billion annually devoted to new construction projects, about 6 million Americans build careers in this industry. This website, sponsored by the Association of Equipment Distributors, the Association of Equipment Manufacturers, and Associated General Contractors, introduces an interesting array of construction-related professions.

Dream It Do It *www.dreamit-doit.com*
In order to make manufacturing a preferred career choice by 2010, the National Association of Manufacturing's Center for Workforce Success is reaching out to young adults and their parents, educators, communities, and policy-makers to change their minds about manufacturing's future and its careers. This website introduces high-demand 21st-century manufacturing professions many will find surprising and worthy of serious consideration.

Get Tech *www.gettech.org*
Another award-winning website from the National Association of Manufacturing.

Take Another Look *www.Nrf.com/content/foundation/rcp/main.htm*
The National Retail Federation challenges students to take another look at their industry by introducing a wide variety of careers associated with marketing and advertising, store management, sales, distribution and logistics, e-commerce, and more.

Index

Page numbers in **boldface** indicate main articles. Page numbers in *italics* indicate photographs.